Bilingual By Choice

Raising Kids in Two (or more!) Languages

Bilingual By Choice

Raising Kids in Two (or more!) Languages

Virginie Raguenaud

nb

NICHOLAS BREALEY
PUBLISHING

BOSTON • LONDON

First published by Nicholas Brealey Publishing in 2009.

Nicholas Brealey Publishing
20 Park Plaza, Suite 1115A
Boston, MA 02116, USA
Tel: + 617-523-3801
Fax: + 617-523-3708

Nicholas Brealey Publishing
3-5 Spafield Street, Clerkenwell
London, EC1R 4QB, UK
Tel: +44-(0)-207-239-0360
Fax: +44-(0)-207-239-0370

www.nicholasbrealey.com

© 2009 by Virginie Raguenaud

Printed in the United States of America

13 12 11 10 09   1 2 3 4 5

ISBN: 978-1-85788-526-2

Library of Congress Cataloging-in-Publication Data
Raguenaud, Virginie.
   Bilingual by choice : raising kids in two (or more!) languages / by
Virginie Raguenaud.
      p. cm.
   ISBN 978-1-85788-526-2
   1. Bilingualism in children.   2. Language acquisition.   3. Multilingualism
in children.   4. Child rearing.   5. Child development.   I. Title.
   P115.2.R34 2009
   404'.2083—dc22

                                                            2009033076

To my parents, Suzy and Jean-Pierre Raguenaud,
for packing up and crossing cultures with three teenagers in tow.

To my daughters Natasha and Sofiya, and my husband Vern,
for continuing this bilingual, nomadic journey with me.

CONTENTS

ACKNOWLEDGMENTS

The idea for this book came during my first presentation at the 2007 Families in Global Transition conference. Many of the parents I met were struggling to keep their school-age children bilingual and looking for solutions. With her enthusiasm and confidence in me, Ruth Van Reken encouraged me to put together a proposal and generously opened the door at Nicholas Brealey Publishing and for that I'm very grateful.

It is daunting to write a book (with three-year old twins at home!) but I could not have had a kinder team to work with. It started with a memorable meeting in Boston with former publisher Patricia O'Hare, Chuck Dresner, and Jennifer Olsen at the onset of a December blizzard. Although it took me six hours to get home on the bus (usually a one-hr. ride!), I still had a huge grin on my face when I finally walked through the door!

Once I finished writing the original manuscript, I worked with two wonderful editors, Wendy Lazear and Kitty Colton, who helped me transform my "stream of consciousness" into a well-organized, easy-to-read manuscript. Thank you, thank you!

To my editor Erika Heilman, I'm grateful for your commitment to this project and your guidance throughout the editorial process.

I also want to thank Nicholas Brealey for ultimately taking a chance on a first-time author.

Although the writing process is fairly lonely, I was inspired by the great work and brilliant minds of Colin Baker, Francois Grosjean, Ellen Bialystok, Fred Genesee, Jim Cummins, Stephen Krasner, Donaldo Macedo, and Ofelia García. Thank you for your commitment to the education of our budding bilingual children.

I'm grateful to all the parents who took the time to answer my questionnaire and who contributed their inspiring stories in personal interviews. To my family and friends, local and global, thanks for your support and insights during the writing process. Finally, I want to thank my husband Vern for the exciting travel adventures during the last seventeen years, for your love and patience, and for supporting me in raising our girls in two (or three!) languages.

FOREWORD

Bilingualism and bi-literacy are admirable goals for every individual. At the National Association for Bilingual Education (NABE), we embrace this mantra and advocate learning more than one language and culture. We are now a global society and we must learn to create unity within diversity.

As tireless advocates who work to influence and create more-inclusive language policies, more bilingual programs, and better teacher training, we know that we are investing in our children's education, our nation's leadership, and our world's well-being. By using our native and second languages in everyday life, we develop intercultural understanding and show, by example, that we respect and can effectively cross cultural and linguistic borders.

Minority language groups are often identified with relatively high unemployment, low pay, poverty, and powerlessness. However, local economies, working with community initiatives, can support and sustain minority languages. Bilingualism is valuable to all as it promotes cultural understanding and gives a competitive edge in an increasing number of vocations. Supporting our native languages is always a good investment!

With this in mind, NABE recommends *Bilingual by Choice* because it is aligned with our mission to mobilize parents and communities to support the education of bilingual and English language learners. As Virginie Raguenaud writes in this book, bilingual children gain intercultural awareness and learn early on that the world is not defined in the same way by other cultural groups. By teaching our children to speak another language and to understand another culture, we are creating a more cooperative generation.

Bilingual By Choice offers crucial information to help parents overcome today's challenges in raising and educating bilingual children. Together, we need to cultivate a multilingual, multicultural society by supporting and promoting policies, programs, pedagogy, and research that yield academic success, value native language, lead to English proficiency, and respect cultural and linguistic diversity.

This practical book offers important strategies that can be implemented right away by parents to make sure that their children become active and contributing participants in this world. It explains the benefits of bilingualism, shows parents how to raise and keep their children bilingual, addresses the cultural challenges at home, and helps parents commit to bi-literacy to ensure their children's academic success.

As former NABE parent representative and Vice-President, I encourage parents and educators to read *Bilingual By Choice* and to experience all the positive effects bilingualism offers to our world today.

Rossana Ramírez-Boyd, Ph. D.
Parent Representative 2001–2003
former Vice-President 2008–2009, National Association for Bilingual
  Education

INTRODUCTION

A shift is happening right now. Powerful institutions are coming to realize that people who speak a second language, and understand different cultural nuances, make great contributions to this country in national security, diplomacy, international business, health care, the arts, education, tourism, and many other areas.

This shift in perception is going to help us as we commit to raising our children with two languages. It will mean more support from our schools and our communities as we help our children sustain their first language and excel in English. But our children's bilingual future—with all its life-changing social, academic, and economic benefits—will require a high level of commitment and creativity on our part. We still need to expose many misconceptions about childhood bilingualism and second-language acquisition.

In a recent interview, linguist and Professor Emeritus at the University of Southern California, Dr. Stephen Krashen said, "Bilingualism in the U.S. only has a future if it is explained to the public and the research becomes well known." When I started my master's in intercultural relations, I came across extensive research on the identity development of bicultural and bilingual children that finally gave me a clearer picture of what I had lived through as a twelve-year-old newcomer from France.

But I also realized that this valuable information rarely leaves academic circles and rarely reaches the people who, like me, desperately need it to make sense of their uprooted childhoods.

This book is my attempt to share the knowledge. As you follow the text, you will see that my bicultural identity shows up regularly. The French side of me likes to listen to the experts and quietly take notes. I get inspired by their efforts to advance the cause of bilingual children. The American side of me likes to engage in a more spirited form of learning: honest insights from parents, who can expose all the complexities—and sometimes frustrations—of raising bilingual children. In the mix, I have also added my own narrative of my relocation to the U.S. and how my mother—born and raised in Belgium—and my father—born and raised in Madagascar—succeeded in raising three "late" bilingual and multicultural daughters.

When I decided to raise my twin daughters, Natasha and Sofiya, bilingually, I came across several books that focused on the logistics of creating a bilingual environment at home: Who will speak what language? How much exposure will the children get? But my conversations with other parents made me realize that we had to take it a step further, looking deeply at the obstacles and finding out why certain families were successful at raising bilingual children and why many failed.

I also wanted to explore the cultural issues in our lives that cannot be ignored. For most of us, bilingualism is not just about raising children to speak two languages. It's also about raising bicultural children who learn early on that there are different ways to see the world and different perspectives about what's right and wrong; children who come to know that our truths are just that—ours. Bicultural children gain intercultural awareness and learn early on that the world as they know it is not being defined in the same ways by other cultural groups. By teaching our children to speak another language and to understand another culture, we're creating a smarter and more cooperative generation.

The subject of bilingualism in this country, unfortunately, often turns into a political discussion of race and power because not everyone is given access to the resources needed to excel in two languages. In some circles the push for bilingualism is also grossly misinterpreted as immigrants' desire to to sustain their first language at the expense of English. That's not the case. Immigrants are learning English much faster than their predecessors because they understand that it leads to extraordinary opportunities. However, many of us also know that if our children acquire our native language, in addition to learning English, they will have a brighter future.

Although more than 54 million of us speak a language other than English at home, this country is still defined as monolingual. That's puzzling, since even our Founding Fathers were multilingual! Benjamin Franklin spoke six languages, including English, French, Spanish, German, Italian, and Latin. Thomas Jefferson could read Greek, Latin, French, Spanish, and Italian. He often wrote to friends about the importance of speaking foreign languages to better connect with the rest of the world—a message we should all pass on to our children.

The reality today is that this country needs well-educated bilingual and biliterate Americans in almost every field, at the national, state, and local levels—from the National Security Agency, recruiting individuals with language skills in Arabic, Chinese, Dari, Farsi, Pashtu, Russian, Sub-Saharan African, Turkish, and Urdu, to our public schools, which face a critical shortage of qualified bilingual teachers. If there's a time to give bilingualism a future, it's now. Like it or not, globalization is here to stay; we might as well make it work for us!

CHAPTER 1

Getting Past the Misconceptions About Bilingualism

Ethnic and national conflicts are most often precipitated when nation-states ignore demands for greater cultural and linguistic democracy, not—as is commonly assumed—when they accommodate them.

Stephen May, author of *Language and Minority Rights*

A Conscious Choice

As a bilingual mom-to-be, I was curious to see which language would feel most natural when I first met my twin girls. Although I associate French with family and nurturing, English has been my community language for the last twenty-seven years. I've spoken English in my graduate studies, my work, and my twelve-year marriage. For some bilingual parents, the language choice is not always obvious and sometimes only reveals itself the first time we hold our children. On our first day together in the hospital, the girls and I found ourselves bonding in French, and we've continued to do so ever since. I have to say, speaking French in the delivery room felt especially sweet and intimate with a nine-member crew of doctors, nurses, and an anesthesiologist working around us! (Twin deliveries create quite a commotion!)

Raising a bilingual child—either from birth or after relocation—is a necessity for many parents. We want to keep family ties intact and share our cultural selves with our children. However, as parents we have to make a conscious choice to *keep* our children bilingual. It's a common misconception that children will simply pick up languages if they're exposed to them. It takes commitment and creativity at home and in our communities for children to learn and, more importantly, maintain two languages. Which is probably why we all know at least one adult who's expressed regret at having lost a parent's native language. I believe we can succeed if we pay attention to the research, if we listen to the insights of successful bilingual adults, and if we learn as a family to mindfully integrate our native language and our cultural traditions in our daily lives.

EARLY SKILLS

To start, the research reminds us that learning two languages from birth is as natural as hearing and speaking only one language. McGill University Professor Fred Genesee, a well-respected scholar in childhood bilingualism, found that infants are able to discriminate between the sounds of two languages from a very early age, months before they can produce any sounds. Studies show that even the babbling of infants is language specific. (1) An infant with a Spanish father and an English-speaking mother will use Spanish sounds with his father and English sounds with his mother.

Research shows that the ability to hear different phonetic pronunciations is sharpest before the age of three. (2) Infants and toddlers can differentiate a wider variety of language sounds than older children. Under normal circumstances, children who are exposed to two languages from birth will learn to speak them with a native accent. Although everyone, at any age, should be encouraged to learn a second language, the biggest difference between children's and adult's bilingual development will be the ability to develop native-like pronunciation.

Another early benefit is the development of metalinguistic awareness as children learn to differentiate early on the two language systems used and understand that there are two (or more) words to name one particular object. (3) Before their second birthday, Natasha and Sofiya made the connection that French and English represented two separate languages.

As I sat Natasha down one day in her highchair and wrapped the belt around her waist, she looked at me and said, "Papa says seatbelt . . . *Maman dit ceinture.*" Even though I'm not a linguist, I could feel at that moment that something amazing was happening in her brain as she reflected on our home's language mix. Out of curiosity I quizzed her further and asked what *she* said. Natasha without hesitation replied "Belt!" while Sofiya smiled at me and said, "*Ceinture, Maman.*" (They like to contradict one another, so with twins I'm guaranteed at least one answer in French!)

According to well-known Canadian scholar Ellen Bialystok, author of *Language Processing in Bilingual Children*, this ability to reflect on language as a system is "a crucial component of cognitive development because of its documented relation to language ability, symbolic development, and literacy skills." This awareness often leads to a stronger appreciation for reading. (4) Children who are exposed to two languages learn to think about language and analyze it, the way travelers to another country start to think about their own behaviors and assumptions. This flexibility and creativity show up in clever ways as our children learn to speak and strengthen their budding bilingual cognitive skills. In these captivating early stages of language development, we're witnessing what will soon be an exceptional language repertoire that will give them unique ways to express themselves and better communicate with the world around them.

Unfortunately, personal language choices and the benefits of early bilingualism are often overshadowed by negative misconceptions generated in the media, in schools, and in communities at large. It's impossible to discuss bilingualism in the U.S. without encountering fear, ignorance, and prejudice. It's important for parents who are reluctant to raise their children with two languages to understand the ways in which certain aspects of childhood bilingualism are misinterpreted or exaggerated. We must also be aware that our own attitudes and beliefs play a crucial role in helping our children sustain their languages as they grow. For example, if a parent has been made to believe that his native language is less relevant than English, his child will soon believe that message as well.

To make sure that our children reap all the lifelong cultural, social, and economic benefits of speaking two languages, let's look at how scientific research objectively dispels the most common misconceptions of early bilingualism.

Language Delay

Not all children develop language at the same rate—a fact that sometimes confuses parents who relate language delay to their bilingual choice. In our personal experience there was a wide gap between Natasha's and Sofiya's language development. Natasha spoke two- and three-word combinations well before her second birthday, while Sofiya developed other skills and began two- and three-word combinations at around two-and-a-half years old. At first, we wondered why Sofiya wasn't speaking as much as her sister. But we noticed that she was making progress nonetheless, adding new words to her vocabulary and following directions, so we decided to focus on what she *was* accomplishing in her own right instead of comparing her to her sister. Once we had made the decision to raise our girls bilingually—to understand different perspectives, to communicate and think creatively in two languages, to connect with people from diverse backgrounds—it seemed trivial to worry about whether they said their first words at 9 months or at 15 months!

When you read about language-delay issues from parents from different cultures, it soon becomes obvious that everyone—family, neighbors, pediatricians—bases their comments on cultural values that represent only one perspective. In her book *How Language Comes to Children*, psycholinguist Benedicte de Boysson-Bardies explains that, in general, "American mothers encourage their child to talk and, above all, to name . . . . while French mothers do not watch for linguistic performances, feeling instead that the child ought to be happy and well behaved and should play a great deal." She adds, "Thus, too, German mothers expect their children to speak later than do Costa Rican mothers." (5) Of course these are generalizations but they point to the central role culture plays in children's language development. Parents around the world obviously have different expectations for their children.

Because of the emphasis in our U.S. culture on "doing everything early," the term *language delay* is often misunderstood. There is such a wide time frame for reaching each language milestone that parents unwillingly find themselves comparing their children's development with other children around them. Even with the best intentions, it's difficult not to! However, according to the American Speech-Language-Hearing Association, only three to ten percent of children will experience language delays. (6) Here are the association's general guidelines for parents raising bilingual children: "Like other children, most bilingual children speak their first words by the time they are one year old (e.g., "mama" or "dada"). By age two, most bilingual children can use two-word phrases (e.g., "my ball" or "no juice"). These are the same language developmental milestones seen in children who learn only one language." (7) Most speech pathologists and pediatricians agree that parents should watch for the more serious symptoms to keep things in perspective. They include:

- not babbling by 12 to 15 months
- not understanding simple commands by 18 months
- not talking by the age of two
- not using sentences by the age of three
- not being able to tell a simple story by the age of four or five (8)

In 2002, cognitive neuroscientist Laura-Ann Petitto and her colleague Ioulia Kovelman looked at different stages of brain development and matched them with four different time frames of bilingual language exposure. They concluded that early and extensive exposure to a second language is beneficial for brain development. According to Petitto, "This will occur without any of the dreaded 'language contamination' often attributed to early bilingual exposure." (9)

Although it often is the most pressing issue for new parents raising bilingual children, there is simply no scientific data that proves that hearing and speaking two languages from birth will cause a language delay. As the American Speech-Language-Hearing Association stipulates, "Children all over the world learn more than one language without developing speech or language problems. Bilingual children develop language skills just as other children do." (10)

ENOUGH LANGUAGE EXPOSURE?

Language delay may occur, however, if a child has sparse exposure to one of his languages. For example, if the parent who speaks the home language is also away at work most often, it will take much family and community support and resources to make sure the child hears and speaks that language enough with other adults and peers to reach the desired level of fluency. If parents worry about how much exposure their children are getting in the home language, the first step, according to researchers, is to get a detailed picture of how much daily input they receive in and outside the home. It's like figuring out how much you spend a month—until you write it all down, you don't realize that daily café latte is costing you $800 a year!

Although researchers have not agreed on the minimum amount of exposure needed for a child to master a language, they agree that parents will be more successful if they monitor the situation carefully. According to Professor Genesee, "Children are capable of learning two languages at the same time at the same rate as monolingual children provided they get continuous and rich exposure to both over an extended period of time." (11) Parents need to provide their children with daily opportunities to learn and repeat a rich and varied vocabulary. It's clear that if a child has sparse or sporadic exposure to one of his languages, he will not meet the expected milestones in language acquisition and is less likely to become bilingual.

CONSISTENCY

Language delay may also occur if a parent unexpectedly switches from one language to another, especially when the child is under age six. (12) This can happen following a relocation, for example, or because of pressure from school officials to drop the home language. The language we use to identify the world around us, and to communicate our feelings, our beliefs, and our values, is difficult to change without causing damage to the emotional bond we've created with our children. Tracey Tokuhama-Espinosa, author of *Raising Multilingual Children*, describes her personal experience with abruptly changing languages. When her youngest son was one-year-old, the family moved from Ecuador to Boston, and Tokuhama-Espinosa decided to switch from English to Spanish, to give the minority language more exposure.

Tokuhama-Espinosa and her husband spoke English together in the community, but spoke only Spanish at home. The consequences were quite alarming. In her book, the author reports that her son's second year basically consisted of animal sounds, with very few words in the mix.

It was only after another move to Ecuador, then Switzerland, when the family had switched back to their original plan, with Tokuhama-Espinosa speaking English again at home, that their son, at age three, started to figure out his language environment. Based on her personal experience and her extensive research, Tokuhama-Espinosa concluded, "Switching languages on a small child, especially with everything else being changed at the same time (house, school, friends, food) can create great confusion and cause extreme stress and even rejection of the language, the country, and the parent." (13)

Since each child is unique and each family has its own way of being, parents ultimately will know if something doesn't feel right in their child's language development. It's important to note that if you suspect a hearing problem or a potential disorder, it's always better to consult with a pediatrician who can recommend a bilingual speech therapist or a counselor for proper evaluation. If there is an issue, the earlier it's detected, the better.

Semilingualism

When well-meaning people find out that you're planning to raise your children in two languages, they may express concern that your strategy could lead to semilingualism—a lack of proficiency in either language as compared to monolingual children. Semilingualism means your children may have a smaller vocabulary, poor grammar, or trouble expressing complex thoughts and creativity. (14) It's easy to see how the issue of semilingualism could be used to discourage or scare parents who wish to pass on their native language to their children. No parent wants their children to be "deficient" in their languages. However, most experts agree that fears of semilingualism are misguided. As Professor Ulrike Jessner, author of *Linguistic Awareness in Multilinguals*, explains, "Multilinguals are still seen as multiple monolinguals in one, which most of the time necessarily leads to the treatment of multilinguals as incompetent speakers in each of their languages." (15)

SOCIAL AND POLITICAL PRESSURES

As more and more research is conducted on how bilinguals use their extensive language skills, scholars are realizing that semilingualism, or comparing language proficiency of bilinguals to monolinguals, is not helpful. The social and political power issues at work are obvious when, for instance, monolinguals mention semilingualism in connection with immigrants who want to maintain their native language, but not in connection with the education of children of diplomats.

It is more beneficial for our children's critical language development to discuss ways in which parents, schools, and communities can work together to help young bilinguals enrich their vocabulary in both languages with more activities, books, and language programs.

If a child experiences a language delay in one of his languages, it can often be traced to an economic, social, or educational factor. Researchers agree that with better opportunities in school, better resources for teachers, less racism and discrimination, and more societal support for foreign languages, a child can learn to speak two languages. Instead of focusing on semilingualism as a reason not to encourage bilingualism, we're better off finding ways to get children past the stage of poor grammar or low vocabulary.

We need to give children access to more books and encourage more parents to read with their children on a daily basis.

BALANCED BILINGUALISM?

Balanced bilingualism is a myth. Bilinguals use their languages in different situations, to discuss different topics; therefore they will never have the exact same proficiency in both languages. But even bilingual adults struggle with this unrealistic pressure to speak both languages perfectly. Bilinguals sometimes feel inferior to monolinguals—one mom calling herself "lazy"—when they struggle to express themselves in one of their languages. We can be hard on ourselves, but we can always improve our language skills, and we don't need to belittle our accomplishments as bilinguals and all the cultural, social, and economic benefits we have acquired along the way. Although I identify myself as bilingual, I'm probably described as semilingual by some of my French relatives. For example, most of my research, writing, and studies on the subject of childhood bilingualism have been in English. So when I discuss this book with my French relatives, I do struggle to explain it all in French. On the other hand, in English I've struggled with basic vocabulary words while playing the board game Pictionary, believe it or not, which always makes my in-laws hesitate to be on my team! For some reason, I just never learned the words "gangplank," "paddy wagon," or "matterhorn."

Everyone differs in their language proficiency, regardless of how many languages we speak. The focus of the conversation should be on how we can improve our skills and our children's skills as bilinguals, rather than on whether we should drop one language for fear of semilingualism. It also helps when we do our part as parents to better educate the people around us—friends, co-workers, teachers—about what it means to us to be bilingual, how we use our languages in different circumstances, and the important role that bilingualism plays in our familial and social relationships.

Language Overload

Even those of us who understand the benefits of bilingualism and whole-heartedly wish to pass on our native language to our children sometimes suffer a lingering fear that we're overloading our young children's brains. We worry because we're looking at the situation from an adult's perspective. We inadvertently underestimate our children's ability to learn. But if we approach language learning in the same loving and gentle way in which we encouraged their first steps and their first drawings, we don't need to worry. Every piece of empirical evidence I have found on the subject—U.S.-based and international—shows that, under normal circumstances, children can learn two (or more) languages, naturally and effortlessly, *if they need them to communicate.*

The brain of a child is remarkably malleable, according to scientists, and it provides significant clues to the development of a second or third language. A group of neurologists who studied the brains of children who experienced a stroke around the ages of six and seven found that, surprisingly, language development was not affected but was actually rerouted to a different part of the brain. For an adult, on the other hand, the same kind of injury will often cause a permanent loss of language. (16) This startling evidence of the brain's plasticity in early childhood helps explain why, under normal circumstances, young children are capable of handling a second or third language without being burdened by it. As bilingual speech-language pathologist Grace Libardo Alvarez concludes, "Infants have a biological capacity for multilingualism." (17)

There are a few things parents can keep in mind when they feel anxious about language overload:

- Don't try to speed things up—let your child's language development happen naturally, as you did when you watched him take his first steps.

- Talk to other parents with older bilingual children and learn from their experience.

- Don't project your own difficulties in learning a second or third language onto your child's language development.

- Stay positive and enthusiastic. Our own attitudes and assumptions will greatly influence how our children approach language learning. Encouragement and optimism can go a long way.

Theodore Andersson, author of *A Guide to Family Reading in Two Languages*, believes that "We grossly underestimate the capacities of children." He offers this advice: "By observing their own children closely, by responding fully to their questions, and by surrounding them with interesting materials and activities, parents can learn something of their children's potential and refrain from inhibiting their learning by limiting their expectations." (18)

Some people argue that children of low socioeconomic status have enough hardships and shouldn't be burdened with the extra demands of bilingualism. Their concern may be well-meaning but it's a devastating misconception.

Everywhere we can see the economic, cultural, educational, and social benefits of sustaining a first language while learning English. Our world languages create and reinforce our ties to our families and to our language communities and contribute to our social and psychological well-being. For children who relocate to a new culture, the home language can become their lifeline that helps them connect their past to the present. Maintaining their native language gives them a better sense of who they are and where they come from.

When we encourage young children—of all socioeconomic groups—to develop both languages, we're not just helping them integrate their different cultural selves; we're also guiding them toward more academic success, healthy social relationships with both cultural groups, more tolerance and acceptance toward other people, and a stronger financial future. As author Tokuhama-Espinosa reminds us, "A child's life experiences up to age seven form her treasure chest of neuro-connections. What she has been lucky enough to hear, smell, taste, touch, and see up to this point are the basis for all future learning." (19) (I like to remind myself about that every time I'm about to embark on another international flight with two preschoolers!)

Special Needs

New parents often have a lingering fear that exposing our children to two or more languages will somehow lead to unnecessary stress and potentially cause language disorders. A *Science Daily* article from September 2008 was headlined "Bilingual children more likely to stutter." In fact, the research in the article doesn't show that bilingualism causes stuttering, but the authors conclude that children would benefit from waiting to learn a second language because ". . . this reduces the chance of starting to stutter and aids the chances of recovery later in childhood." (20)

The problem with this kind of research is that it often overlooks the social, emotional, and cultural factors surrounding each child, and thus creates misleading information. For me, reading this article was like being told that it's not prudent to have twins because there are risks involved. My reality is that the benefits far outweigh the risks. When it comes to languages (and children!), I can't live with just one. Natasha and Sofiya also need two languages in order to communicate with their two families.

It's true that there are bilinguals who stutter, but the research does not prove that learning two languages from birth is the cause. Among many research findings, an extensive survey done at the world-renowned University College London concluded that "There is no difference between monolingual and bilingual speakers in terms of their likelihood of having stuttering in their life." (21)

UNDERSTANDING STUTTERING

First, experts emphasize that stuttering in children—or disruptions in their speech—as they learn to communicate is common and is considered a normal phase of language development. (22) According to the National Stutter Association, children will typically start to stutter between the ages of two-and-a-half and five, and about five percent of children stutter. Although there are no known causes for stuttering and no simple cure for it, many children can greatly improve their speech with the help of a specialist. In addition, according to the NSA, "Recent research shows that as many as three out of four children who show signs of early stuttering will recover within the first year or so after they start stuttering." (23)

Instead of asking if bilingualism causes stuttering, a more helpful question, perhaps, is: How can we as parents help our children if they start to stutter? As parents we can find ways to keep our languages alive without causing a heightened sense of anxiety in our children. Even when parents feel they have to "force" their children to speak the home language, for fear that the community language will take center stage, it's important to keep it light-hearted and gentle. A child should never be scolded or punished when it comes to developing language skills.

Researchers agree that our approach, attitude, and expectations as parents greatly influence the process of raising bilingual children. Childhood bilingualism expert Barbara Abdelilah-Bauer, author of the book *Le Defi des Enfants Bilingues* (The Challenge of Bilingual Children), recommends that parents who see symptoms of stuttering in their bilingual children should ease the language rules around the house and follow the child's lead in terms of which language he prefers to use to express himself. (24) It makes sense to reduce the pressure and tension around a child who stutters; to speak clearly in front of the child; and to not make her feel self-conscious in any way. The solution is not, however, to give up speaking our home language, but rather to become more flexible with our expectations.

EARLY DETECTION

When it comes to all language disorders, early detection is key. Parents who believe in their gut that something is wrong need to speak with a specialist. As you search for the right psychologist or speech language pathologist, make sure that this person understands childhood bilingualism and takes your language background into consideration. According to Professor Colin Baker, author of *The Care and Education of Young Bilinguals*, to get an accurate diagnosis, "Assessment of the child must be completed in both or all languages, using tests normed on bilinguals, and avoiding comparison with monolinguals in phonology, vocabulary, syntax, and fluency." (25)

Unfortunately, misdiagnosis is fairly common. Parents need to stay informed and alert, and ask for a second opinion if need be. Bilingual speech pathologist Deborah Jill Chitester notes that in her profession, "Hispanic origin is often inappropriately referred to as bilingual." She explains, "In my experience, teachers and parents misuse the word when speaking about second-language children who are in the process of acquiring English. This often occurs in bilingual speech evaluations that are conducted by those without proper training . . . . The first line will read: 'This bilingual male only speaks Spanish . . . .' Bilingual means near native communicative competence in both languages, so this statement contradicts itself." (26)

The repercussions of a misdiagnosis are obviously enormous, considering that the most common recommendation parents receive is to drop the home language to make the problem go away. For most of us, that's simply not an option. One mom, Dr. Aurore Adamkiewicz, author of *Beyond Natural Cures*, is happy she didn't give up on her languages. She shares her poignant story:

> We raised our kids trilingually and we had issues with our oldest one. We were "attacked" by our families, who insisted we were "ruining" our children with language . . . up until then, my husband's family

had insisted we were hurting our children with "healthy food!" Well, it turns out my son was autistic, and it had nothing to do with the languages . . . or whole-grain bread. . . . I will say, though, that our efforts were not in vain. . . . My son, when he started talking at 6, was able to remember all of the different languages and music I had taught him! He was the youngest American invited to study at Interlochen (Center for the Arts), at 8 years old; this is something that we would never have imagined. It was all there in his head—tucked away. It was a little jewel for me. (27)

Professor Baker, along with other well-respected scholars, concludes that it is "very unlikely that bilingualism is linked with, or a direct cause of, the following special needs: visual or hearing impairment, learning disabilities such as dyslexia and developmental aphasia, severe subnormality in cognitive development, behavioral problems and physical handicaps. Membership in a language minority may *coexist* with such conditions, but does not determine them." (28)

Taking Charge

Bilingualism in the U.S. is a tough sell. There are widespread misconceptions—unnecessary distractions—that too often mislead parents who have the ability and the language resources to give their children the gift of bilingualism but who hesitate, or, worse, turn their backs on their home language. The first time I saw Dr. Tove Skutnabb-Kangas's book *Linguistic Genocide in Education—or Worldwide Diversity and Human Rights?* I was taken aback by the blunt title. But as I talked to parents, and as I read U.S.-based and international literature on bilingualism, I realized that we are truly robbing families if we take away their language and cultural rights. Sometimes it's done at the federal level, through language policies and cutbacks on bilingual programs.

Sometimes it's at the local level; for instance, school administrators may tell a parent that if she continues to speak Arabic at home, her child will be placed in special education classes. I also realized that parents should not underestimate the power they have to success-fully raise bilingual and multicultural children, even if their communities are not in sync yet.

Ultimately it's up to us as parents to make it happen. When a potential problem or worry creeps up, trust your instincts. You know what's best for your child. You know when your child is hungry. You know when she needs a hug. You know what she needs to be happy before anyone else around her does. Every day, when you choose to speak and read to her in your native language, you strengthen an intimate bond with her, you expose her to more and more vocabulary, you pique her curiosity with fun and creative activities, and you open her eyes to meaningful cultural traditions and values that are important to your family. You create a treasure chest in your own home. Through it all, remember that her knowledge of languages and her rich cultural heritage mean that the world will soon open up to her.

CHAPTER 2

The Logistics of Raising Bilingual Children

In the total sociocultural environment, it is the parents, especially the mothers and their childrearing practices, who have been proven to have the greatest influence.

Professor Cigdem Kagıtcıbasi, Koc University Rumelifeneri Yolu, Istanbul, Turkey

Defining Your Goals

When we decide to raise our children with two languages, it's helpful to define our goals and priorities and then share them with our families and close friends. We need to ask ourselves: Do I want my children to simply be able to communicate with our family? Do I want them to be able to read and write in the home language? Might they someday pursue their studies in the language? If so, how can I provide access to academic vocabulary? What can I do to help them become bicultural? Can I give them firsthand exposure to my native culture?

Can I make the time to read to them every day? What resources—books, music, language schools, immersion programs, and cultural events—are available to us in the community or on the Internet?

My family's personal goal is for our girls to one day be able to speak, read, and write fluently in French and English. We need all the support we can get to help the children maintain and progress in French. It sometimes means reminding visiting relatives and friends to speak French around the children, even if it's tempting for them to practice their English when they come to the U.S.!

According to Francois Grosjean, author of *Life with Two Languages*, "Children do not acquire (or only partly acquire) the minority language if there isn't community or educational support, or other motivational factors that make using the language a natural thing." During an interview about his personal family situation, Professor Grosjean alluded to the dilemma we all face. "Although we wanted our children to be bilingual," he writes, "living in an English environment like the United States made this very difficult." (1) His family lived here decades ago, but his comment still holds true today.

Global migration is working in our favor, however. The 2007 American Community Survey states that one in five people living in the U.S. speaks a language other than English at home; that's more than 54,000,000 people. (2) We should be able to create abundant speaking opportunities just by getting together with our neighbors! And the numbers are growing every year. The goal is to build a strong support network that includes family and friends, to speak up about our goals for our children's future, and to explain why it's important to expand their minds by passing on our native language and culture.

Language Strategies

ONE LANGUAGE—ONE ENVIRONMENT

The common language strategy One Language One Environment often appeals to parents who share the same native language at home. It guarantees children constant and uninterrupted exposure when both parents fully commit to speaking only their native language when they step over their home's threshold. Irene A. Marquez, founder of Los Bilingual Writers, believes that her parents' resolution was a key factor in helping her become bilingual. She writes, "[I] would come in and I'd start telling her about my day at school, and she'd completely ignore me, as if I wasn't there. My mother and my father both spoke English, but my mother insisted that we speak Spanish at home. So immediately I would have to switch. I'd walk in the door, and I'd immediately go into Spanish. I'd walk back out the door, and immediately go into English. And that's how most of us become bilingual. . . . In Spanish we have a saying that the person who speaks two languages is as good as two people." (3)

The first few years at home, before preschool or kindergarten starts, is the best time to give your child a solid foundation in your native language. Some parents might worry about their child's level of English when it comes time to head off to school, but the reality is that children are eager and motivated to learn their classmates' language and will quickly reach the same level. The first weeks or months at school can include extra assistance from a compassionate teacher to help with the transition, but it's clear that if you choose to live in the U.S. permanently, English will very quickly become your children's dominant language. But they can never get back those first few years at home of consistent exposure to your native language.

ONE PARENT ONE LANGUAGE

In multilingual marriages, the One Parent One Language method is often the preferred strategy. Sometimes both parents each share their minority language with the children, and English is introduced later on in the community and in school as a third language. Or, as is the case in our household, one parent speaks a minority language and the other parent speaks the community language. OPOL establishes clarity and gives the child distinct boundaries. Common sense tells us that it might be easier for a child to keep her languages separate if she can identify one parent with one language. This strategy struck me as wise when Natasha, at age two-and-a-half, made a game of repeating every single word I said throughout the day. It's clear that if I had mixed my languages then, she would have mixed English and French in the same sentences as well. Children do love to repeat everything we say!

The main advantage of OPOL is that it helps parents balance the amount of language input. It's hard to keep track of how much language exposure our children are getting when we're busy multitasking and keeping everyone fed, clean, and happy. This method provides the best assurance that your native language is not overshadowed by the dominant language of the community. I don't know about you, but I don't want to start drawing charts to figure out if my children are hearing enough of my native language. I find it easier to simply speak French to them every day. The reality is, if we truly believe that their lives will be richer if they fully embrace their family's cultural and linguistic backgrounds, then we need to do our part and integrate our native language into our daily activities. When we create a deep emotional bond with our children in one language, it often feels awkward and unnatural to suddenly continue that relationship in a different language. (Bonding in our language will serve us well when obstacles come up during the school years!)

Although research shows—and parents will tell you—that children respond well to One Parent One Language because of its consistency, for some multilingual families it's difficult to keep languages separate. Being bilingual is more complicated than turning on one language while turning off the other one. Even scholars struggle to agree on the best language practices for encouraging bilingualism. In fact, there *is* no perfect strategy. It's complex; strong social, cultural, and political factors come into play. Even when families follow OPOL, languages inevitably mix, since we often use a different language with our partner than with our children. At home I try not to mix languages, but English does creep in once in a while, especially when the four of us are having a conversation together. As one parent explained, "In general, it's one parent-one language, but life is life, and it often gets mixed up." (4)

The good news: many parents report that they mixed languages from the start, and their children still managed to become bilingual with no traumatic aftermath. As Professor Genesee explains, even if parents mix languages, most children will learn to separate their languages if most of the people they come in contact with—relatives and people in the community—speak only one language at a time. (5)

In the end, the most important guideline when deciding on a language strategy is to choose what feels the most natural to both parents, and then support one another steadfastly in your decision. (Even if your in-laws, or your friends, or your child's preschool staff don't agree! It seems everyone around us will have an opinion—as you might have already noticed.) All bilingual children and adults have times when one language takes center stage, times when we find creative ways to incorporate both languages in our lives, and times when we need to work harder to progress in the weaker language. The important thing for parents is to start speaking our native language from day one and keep it relevant in our daily lives in fun and enriching ways.

When Children Mix Languages

Mixing languages is an emotionally charged topic, and there have been entire books dissecting the subject. You will quickly find that everyone has a personal opinion on mixing languages, or code-switching, as it's sometimes referred to in the research. Some parents see it as a normal phase of language development, some find it cognitively or socially inappropriate, and others live in communities where it has become the norm.

Scholars in general don't seem nearly as worried about the subject as young parents are. As Professor Grosjean reminds us, bilingual children will be creative and play with their languages the same way monolingual children do as they develop their language skills. (6) They're learning to express themselves, and they just happen to have more resources at their disposal.

To evaluate why a child mixes her languages, you have to examine the whole picture. There are many variables to consider, including the child's learning style, her age, her personality, her aptitude for languages, how much you mix languages at home, and how you correct her when she uses the "wrong" word. To better understand the situation, here is a list of reasons that children sometimes mix their languages, either in the same sentence or in the same conversation.

Common Reasons for Code-Switching
- Hasn't learned the corresponding vocabulary word yet
- The word has just been used and is easier to remember
- Uses the word in one language more often
- Personal preference
- Wants to get your attention
- The word has specific cultural meaning in one language and not in the other
- Wants to express her bilingual identity

- Aware that the person she's speaking with is bilingual
- Relates an emotion that is linked to a particular language
- Wants to exclude someone from the conversation
- Chooses the shortest word out of pure laziness (my case as a teenager!)

CORRECTING

When children are still at home and just learning to identify their two language systems, mixing languages is usually temporary. I think every parent has to decide what feels most natural in their daily interactions, but it's clear that if we correct a young child every time she says a word in the "wrong" language, we risk taking the spontaneity out of learning and giving her a serious complex. If Sofiya shows me, with great excitement, her new Play-Doh creation and says, "*Regarde, Maman*, octopus!" ("Look, Mom, octopus!") I simply reply, "*Bravo! Quelle belle pieuvre!*" ("What a beautiful octopus!") I give her the French word in my reply, but I don't correct her. I can tell she likes to say the word *octopus*. But later, when I ask her to show me "*la pieuvre*" in a French book, she points at it without hesitation. The objective is to make sure the word is not missing from her vocabulary, or, if it is, to find a fun way to teach it to her.

WHO SPEAKS WHAT?

Mixing languages often happens when young children are still figuring out who's bilingual and who's not. When Natasha and Sofiya were just learning to speak, they assumed that both sets of grandparents could read French books with them. That assumption was usually followed with a puzzled look and a head tilt that said, "What do you mean you can't read this baby book, Nanny?" When children develop a solid understanding of their two language systems—which can happen as early as age two or three—they start to develop a keen sense of who is bilingual and who isn't, and most of the time they will use the appropriate language in their interactions. Madalena Cruz-Ferreira, author of *Three Is A Crowd? Acquiring Portuguese in a Trilingual Environment*, has seen this in her research and with her own trilingual children. She shares this insight: "The bottom line is that [a child] will sort out both languages and their users in time. I'll give you a preview: the next stage will be that once she associates a language with a person, say, when meeting new people, she will vigorously refuse to use any other language with that person." (7)

HOW TO HELP

Although most researchers agree that mixing languages is a normal and temporary stage of language development, there are a few helpful tips for parents who are still concerned. They can

- refrain from mixing languages themselves in front of the children
- give their children more daily opportunities to expand their vocabulary by reading age-appropriate books together
- engage the children in more varied activities and conversations in both their languages (consider the list in Chapters 9 and 10)
- make sure that the children hear and speak with relatives and people in the community who speak only one language
- correct them by repeating the word in the appropriate language

With some work and perseverance on the parents' part, children can establish distinct language boundaries at home and achieve language consistency at school.

Learning to Read

A common question for parents raising toddlers with two languages is: Which language should our children learn to read first? Research shows that it is best for children to learn to read in their stronger language, whether it's the language spoken at home or the community language. If children learn to read in English first, that doesn't mean that parents shouldn't be reading to them in their native language as well. As York University Professor of Psychology Ellen Bialystok explains, "There's a lot of worry out there about other languages conflicting with a child's ability to learn to read in English, but that's absolutely not the case. Parents should not hesitate to share their native language with their children—it's a gift." (8)

Sometimes unexpected circumstances determine which language our children will read in first. When I was three years old, my family moved to Jeffersonville, Indiana, for one year. My two sisters, at four and five years old, started school and were suddenly learning to speak and read in English, a language they had never heard before. My mom was concerned about my oldest sister Brigitte's literacy development in French, since she would be starting first grade upon our return to France the following school year. She attempted to read to Brigitte in French in the evenings, but after several tries she dropped the project because Brigitte was not responding well. My mom decided to try again when Brigitte's kindergarten year in English was over.

Because of this unexpected one-year relocation, my sister did learn to read in her weaker language. But after she learned to read in English, she was able to transfer those skills to French. My parents spent the summer helping Brigitte to read in French. By the time she started school in France that September, Brigitte read on par with her classmates. Unknowingly, my parents followed the advice researchers give out today. They didn't push Brigitte; they paid attention to her own particular needs and let her lead the way; they stayed flexible and held back their expectations; and, most importantly, they committed to reading every day to put her back on track once she was able to focus on French again.

According to the American Academy of Pediatrics, "Pushing your child to read before she is ready can get in the way of your child's interest in learning. This love of learning cannot be forced." (9) Most children will learn to read by age six or seven. Some children will learn at four or five. A child has to be able to recognize the letters or symbols, their appropriate sounds, and how to put them together to form words in order to start reading. As parents, we can set the stage for this language milestone in a fun and stress-free way:

- We can read baby books in both languages to our children long before they can read.
- We can make family trips to the library. More and more libraries offer books in different languages, as well as picture books of all the countries around the world.
- We can expose our children to books we read when we were young.
- We can put books by their beds.
- We can offer them books as presents.
- We can ask lovely relatives to mail us any new discoveries from overseas!
- We can serve as role models by reading books, magazines, and newspapers in their presence.
- We can support our local libraries. (One easy contribution is to donate books in your native language after your children have outgrown them.)

University of Maryland Professor John Guthrie's extensive research on reading shows that motivating children to read can have life-altering consequences. According to Guthrie's studies, school-age children from low-income families who had little education but who had access to books and were avid readers consistently outperformed students from higher-income families with higher education who were not enthusiastic readers. Professor Guthrie firmly believes that "engaged readers can overcome traditional barriers to reading achievement, including gender, parental education, and income." (10)

Most researchers encourage each parent to read in his or her native language for the same reasons they encourage the One Parent One Language method. It's more effective for parents to read in their stronger language, and it provides consistency for the child. Reading gives children a chance to learn new words we don't use in our everyday conversations, and it's a critical tool for building academic vocabulary. As Una Cunningham-Andersson writes in *Growing Up with Two Languages*, "No amount of visiting the country where the language is spoken or contact with other speakers can hope to give a child as rich a vocabulary and such a mastery of the nuances of the language as a thorough immersion in its children's literature." (11)

Another valuable reason for reading in our native language is the colorful cultural vignettes in well-chosen books that teach our children about where their family comes from. Of course, some books can be read in any language, such as my personal favorite, *Le Petit Prince,* by Antoine St. Exupery. But many other stories need to be read in the original text to capture all the cultural nuances. It would be fascinating to do a comparative study of international children's books to examine all the cultural variations. Sometimes, if you're missing the cultural context, it's difficult to find the story's meaning. For example, we have a children's book from Cambodia that left me puzzled; it involves two young men, a rabbit, a series of threats, and a very big machete! From my perspective it's not cozy bedtime reading, so for now it stays out of reach on the top shelf.

Keep Talking From Day One

One of the most influential factors in our children's bilingual development is how much language they hear every day. Research shows that, on average, we use 16,000 words per day. (12) That means we have the chance to expose our children to an incredible vocabulary, thereby increasing their chances of success in reading and future academic achievements.

Dr. Betty Hart and Dr. Todd Risley conducted a well-known research study that examined the number of words heard and exchanged between parents and children in forty-two families during a two-and-a-half year period. The participants were from high, middle, and low socio-economic groups. The authors recorded long hours of verbal exchanges between parents and children and found that, on average, the child participants with high-income parents heard eleven million words per year, and the participants with low-income parents heard only three million words per year. (13) According to Dr. Hart and Dr. Risley, this discrepancy in how many words infants and toddlers hear from their parents day after day is a crucial factor in understanding why some students do better in school than others.

To provide an enriched language environment for our children, we need to talk! As parents, we need to narrate every single thing we do around the house. Try it. It will feel very natural to some parents; others might find these monologues awkward at first. But remember that, according to the research, the number of words a child hears throughout the day is directly linked to the child's intelligence and vocabulary size. Language is a free resource we all have at our disposal, regardless of our educational or socioeconomic background. The impact is so strong that it makes you want to chat away with your baby as you empty the dishwasher, fold the towels, mop the floor, or put the groceries away. As Dr. Risley explains, the common vocabulary we use at home lays the foundation for the more sophisticated concepts our children will learn later on. Talking to our children and reading to them every day will teach them new vocabulary words, stimulate their creativity, and increase their knowledge. And there's no need to hire an expensive language tutor!

It's also important for children to hear and absorb the richness of a dialogue in our native language. Those of you with fun and lively relatives who are always ready to talk your ear off: you're in luck! If, like me, you don't have any family living near you to engage in animated conversations, the next best thing is the handy online telephone service used with a webcam. Skype (www.skype.com), for example, has become a great resource for many families scattered around the globe. It's one of those technological advances that makes you wonder how you ever survived without it! It has replaced the telephone at our house. Not only is it a great way to provide more language input for children, but it also helps them develop a closer contact with faraway relatives. They can share everyday moments instead of just hearing the big headlines over the telephone. When we use Skype, I feel that I'm not alone in this quest to raise my girls to speak French; the rest of my family can also help me succeed.

Strategies in Public

What about our conversations in public? At some point we all have to figure out what feels most natural. Some parents simply choose to speak their native language at all times, regardless of how their children or other people around them react. It sends a strong message of language pride to the children. Even if the community is not receptive, parents are expressing their personal enthusiasm for the language and its importance in the context of their family. In cities like New York, Miami, and Chicago, bilingual families might not question whether to use their native language in the company of others, mostly because of the large mix of ethnic and linguistic groups who have made a home there. In smaller towns, however, it is still uncommon to hear a foreign language spoken on the streets. In New Hampshire, where I live, English clearly dominates. I have to say, though, now that I pay more attention to the issue, I'm amazed at how often I meet someone in a store, or at an amusement park, or restaurant who speaks another language fluently with his or her family. When I was pregnant, I suddenly saw babies and strollers everywhere I went; now that I speak a foreign language out in public, I suddenly hear other languages everywhere I go!

For some parents, the situation is more complicated for emotional, social, cultural, or sometimes political reasons.

Here are some issues to consider:

- **The child's age** With infants it's often easy to speak the heritage language in public, since the interaction is more private, quieter, and less subject to reactions from others. When children grow up and become more sensitive to other people's reactions, they often prefer to communicate in the dominant language. One parent writes, "From about age four, my children started to pretend to not understand me when others [were] around. After deciding that raising my voice in public in a foreign language was probably not how I wanted to handle it, I chose to stop speaking the language in public." (14) Parents have to choose their own course of action, depending on what they believe is best for the child. This rejection of the heritage language is often a temporary stage, but it should be handled with tact, humor, and thoughtfulness so that the language does not become a negative element in the child's life. As the authors of *Growing Up With Two Languages* remind us, "At a certain age many youngsters find a reason to be ashamed of their parents, even if they do not have another language or come from another country. They may be too rich or too poor or too ugly or too famous or have the wrong car or the wrong clothes or whatever!" (15) Take the rejection with a grain of salt, and either oblige for a while or explain in a calm and reassuring voice why it's important for you to continue speaking your native language. Many parents who've navigated this road believe that children react better when they get simple but truthful explanations about the family's language decisions.

- **The town's threshold for foreign tongues** Some people are uncomfortable in the presence of someone who speaks a different language. They become self-conscious and worry that someone is speaking about them. They feel threatened by the unknown. When there is a dramatic political situation, certain ethnic groups can become targets of anger and even violence. After the attacks of September 11, 2001, many parents were scared to speak Arabic with their children in public for fear of verbal abuse or physical threats. Unfortunately, it's naïve to think we're all safe to speak our heritage language if we so choose. We still have a lot of minds to convince when it comes to linguistic and cultural tolerance. Even though I have seldom felt discriminated against, I don't automatically assume that everyone I encounter in public will be comfortable with my speaking French to Natasha and Sofiya—even though most of the time I'm just rattling off something inconsequential such as, "What? You have to go to the potty now?" or "We're not buying that. Put it back!"

- **Feelings of alienation** Parents who work hard to integrate themselves in their community before they have children sometimes find it difficult to speak their native language in public after the kids come along; suddenly, they find themselves being treated like foreigners all over again. It took me some time to adjust to this feeling when I started speaking French to the girls. Now, when retail clerks ask me if I'm visiting from somewhere, I see it as a chance to raise awareness of the benefits of bilingualism and multiculturalism. They usually end up agreeing, or at least they have an interesting story to tell at their next coffee break! It helps that I have a high level of pride in my French heritage and that I'm comfortable with my bicultural identity.

In some public circumstances, I do speak English. I was once at the playground with Natasha and Sofiya when a young mom struck up a conversation with me. We talked for a while, and then I turned to the girls and said something in French. The woman slowly pulled away from me and started to chat with another parent nearby. I could see that I had made her uncomfortable and had lost an opportunity to get to know someone new. I decided at that moment that I didn't want to isolate myself in this way. I realized that if I wanted to develop new friendships in the community, I would need to speak English at the playground. The key is to decide what works for you personally, and what feels most natural and productive with your friends, acquaintances, neighbors, clerks, and other parents in your community. You don't need to let the community language take over completely; you just need to find a balance that lets you be an active member of your community while you provide enough daily heritage language exposure for your children.

- **Support of Friends** It's important to explain to your close friends—your support network whom you see regularly—what raising bilingual children means to you, how it affects your family, and how valuable their support is, especially if they can be vocal around your children about how great it is to speak two languages. In certain circumstances, to prevent friends or acquaintances from feeling excluded, parents sometimes give a simple translation to let them know what they've just said. It has to come naturally, or else it quickly feels cumbersome. Most of the time, when we're in a group situation, I translate without thinking about it, but I gauge what's important for the rest of the group to know and what I can say to the girls only. For example, I will translate, "Let's all go to the park!" but not "Natasha, can you put the cap back on your marker, please?" Since the day my daughters were born, I've relished being able to talk to them in a language few people around us can understand. Now that they're getting older and have more contact with other children and adults, I'm even more grateful for the bond we've created in French. It adds another intimate layer to our mother-daughter relationship.

- **Personality types** Parents who are introverted and don't want to call attention to themselves may find it difficult to speak the heritage language in a public place when everyone else is speaking the community language. Parents who feel insecure about their native-language skills may also hesitate to speak in front of others, especially if their community does not value their native language. Again, it's about finding what feels natural for you. If you decide to speak the community language in public, you can always compensate with engaging heritage language activities at home or in the company of supportive friends and family. Passing on our heritage language should not be a stressful experience that keeps you up at night with worry. It should be fun and pleasant and full of love, for both parents and children. As one parent writes, "Relax. Parenting is hard enough. By all means listen to advice, but everyone's situation is different. Find your own way. Don't let it be a burden." (16)

Staying Flexible but Committed

Because of the countless variations in each of our lives, these are only general guidelines. We learn from parents who've been through the experience of raising bilingual children, and we learn from the recommendations of researchers; then we develop our own plan. Once we decide on a language strategy, we discuss it with family and friends so that we can get as many people on board as possible. In the U.S. it's still difficult to find entire communities already in place that take a stand on promoting bilingualism for all. So we build our own network. We discuss what's working and what's not working on message boards and chat rooms online. We read books on bilingualism. Most importantly, we commit to speaking our native language every day with our children because it's the most basic ingredient. From that commitment, we build. We read to our children every day; we guide them as they learn to differentiate between their two languages; we get past the worries of mixing languages; and we provide creative and exciting activities in and outside the home to expand our children's vocabulary and their cultural knowledge. As parents, we know our world languages are relevant, but as we'll see in the next chapter, we now have to convince the skeptics: our school-age children.

CHAPTER 3

Introducing a Second Language to a School-Age Child

By our active and committed presence as citizens of different ethnicities, races, traditions, and linguistic backgrounds, we challenge America to expand its understanding and compassion and thus grow stronger as a nation.

Julia Alvarez, author of How the Garcia Girls Lost Their Accents

For some parents, raising bilingual children comes unexpectedly, as the result of a relocation. According to the United Nations, at least 185 million people live in countries other than the one in which they were born, compared to just seventy million three decades ago. (1) This global migration, whether it occurs for economic, political, or social reasons, give parents the chance to expand their children's cultural knowledge, their worldview, and their language skills. My parents, for example, decided to move to the U.S. with three young teenagers to create a new life away from the disappointing political structure in France at the time. My father was working for an international company and was able to transfer to its headquarters in New York. We didn't belong to an expatriate community when we arrived, which meant that we were on our own to figure out how everything worked. As a family, we had had a positive experience eight years earlier with our one-year stay in Jeffersonville, Indiana, which convinced my parents to pack up and move once more.

When children start a new life in a new country, they often experience culture shock. This challenging transition unfortunately does not always get all the attention it deserves. Parents must focus on the immediate survival elements, such as finding proper housing, meeting school administrators, and learning the roadways around the new community, from the bank to the grocery store.

These are the questions we will look at in this chapter: How can parents make relocation a positive and enriching experience for their children? What can the latest research findings teach us? And how do we help our children maintain and progress in their native language *and* learn to speak English fluently?

The lifelong benefits of crossing cultures should far outweigh the difficult moments. But when you're twelve years old, standing in front of a classroom full of strangers who don't speak your language, it all seems insurmountable. Nineteen days after our plane touched down at JFK airport in New York, my sisters and I walked into an American public school, and the world as we knew it disappeared. During one plane ride, I lost the ability to read, speak, express my feelings, question, argue, laugh, and learn—anywhere except inside my home, with my parents and sisters. This harsh reality explains why my heart sinks when I hear anyone—a teacher, a neighbor, a politician—advise parents to give up speaking their native language with their children to (supposedly) give them an edge and help them learn English faster. Our home language was my lifeline, my "thread of continuity," as author Peter Marris describes it in his book *Loss and Change*. It connected my old life with my new, as-yet undecipherable, surroundings. As Marris explains, "The anxiety of venturing into the unknown . . . can be dominated, just because the thread of continuity has not been broken." (2) If my parents had abandoned French and spoken to me only in their broken English, I would have lost my footing on the last solid rock under me and fallen into an abyss.

A long list of problems can arise when school-age children are cut off from their native language. Worldwide research findings have shown that it can damage children's self-esteem, their sense of belonging, the nurturing and emotional bond with their family across the generations, their identity development, their chances of succeeding in their second language, their potential progress in their native language, and their ability to achieve high levels of literacy in both languages. The negative side effects can be felt years later. Abandoning the native language is not a decision to take lightly, and it's certainly not one to be made outside the family unit.

Unfortunately, there are strong societal pressures telling us that our children will not master English if they spend time at home speaking the family language. Parents hesitate and fear hurting their children's academic success. They may have been the victims of racism or discrimination themselves, and they don't want their children to go through the same pain. Or they believe the adjustment will go more smoothly if they erase ties to the past and assimilate to the new culture. Parents sometimes do not see the value of their native language. Or they inadvertently relegate it to the occasional phone calls to grandparents and cousins, or use it only for disciplining the children, and English slowly takes over during the conversations around the dinner table. Every family has its own unique story.

But with the right tools and resources, our children can integrate fully into a new culture without giving up their native language. Children who relocate to a new country benefit immensely from maintaining their native language and cultural heritage. It provides them with a healthy sense of self and confidence and guarantees a smoother, more positive transition as they adjust to their new surroundings and become bilingual and biliterate. It is a must for their academic and professional future, regardless of the family's language. With the direction of the world, economically and politically, there is no sensible reason for a child to be told to leave a language behind. The National Association for Bilingual Education uses a slogan we should all promote: "No Bilingual Child Left Behind!" Realizing the importance of learning a second language, even monolingual families are trying hard, through language classes and private tutors, to offer their children this academic advantage. As parents of children who are raised with two languages, we need to do what we can to keep them moving forward instead of taking two steps back. Those of us who are lucky enough to identify ourselves as bilingual and multicultural adults often have our parents to thank for the doors they opened. Our children will thank us one day as well!

My parents never saw learning languages as a potential burden or a hurdle to our academic learning. Not only did they continue to speak French at home once we moved to the U.S., but they also made sure my sisters and I continued the German lessons we had started in France—on top of having to learn English! What's interesting is that, at the time, I didn't think it was too much to take on. Learning languages seemed as normal and as useful as learning math. But now that I've absorbed and been influenced by this country's language views, I sometimes think, What on earth were they doing to us? There definitely was a strong European influence in my parents' bold move. For historical and geographical reasons, most Europeans tend to respect and value languages and rarely see them as potential obstacles. (As it turned out, signing up for German class also served as a boost to my self-confidence; at the end of my first year in the U.S., it was the only A on my report card!) I think one of the reasons my parents were successful in raising three multilingual daughters is that they made languages a central part of our learning, a subject as important as math or the sciences. As my parents like to point out, there is always a better job prospect for someone who speaks more than one language fluently. Today it is a recognized advantage at any job interview.

Transferring Skills From One Language to Another

There is now solid evidence from a large group of international researchers that children who relocate during their school years with skills in speaking, reading, and writing in their first language will readily transfer their academic knowledge to their second language. Professor Jim Cummins at the University of Toronto has researched this subject for the last thirty years. He came up with the well-supported Linguistic Interdependence Hypothesis, which states that if there is adequate learning in the first language, including reading skills, it will readily transfer to the second language, given sufficient exposure and motivation. (3) Many researchers agree with this view, which promotes building on children's existing skills to help them learn new information. The knowledge that children have acquired in the first language should not be underestimated or dismissed. Total English immersion in the classroom might make sense on a superficial level, but it doesn't allow children to use all of their linguistic and cognitive resources, and it doesn't allow them to be whole.

The fact that children can learn conversational English at a fast rate is often mistaken as a sign that they are now "caught up" and can easily blend into their new curriculum without any more obstacles. Although my sisters and I could communicate in English with our new classmates after four or five months, there were still many subject matters that were clearly out of our grasp. Associate Professor Pauline Gibbons of the University of Technology in Sydney calls this the difference between "playground language" and "classroom language." She explains, "The playground situation does not normally offer children the opportunity to use such language as: *if we increase the angle by 5 degrees, we could cut the circumference into equal parts.* Nor does it normally require the language associated with the higher-order thinking skills, such as hypothesizing, evaluating, inferring, generalizing, predicting, or classifying . . . . Yet . . . without them, a child's potential in academic areas cannot be realized." (4)

Consider this: A monolingual child arrives in school at age five with a certain fluency in his native language and then spends the next thirteen years expanding on his verbal and literacy skills. Why should we expect a new student, who has to absorb the impact of an international relocation, in all its complexities, to master a second language in a year or two? The research indicates that with the right teaching environment and parental involvement, children need, instead, five to seven years to reach a level of academic proficiency. (5)

ESL Classes

Although more and more educators today realize that language is a resource rather than a problem or obstacle to overcome, many ESL students still feel undermined. The language skills of ESL students are often seen as "deficient." People sometimes forget that these students already speak another language fluently and are now *adding* knowledge. Professor Emeritus Donaldo Macedo of the University of Massachusetts in Boston recounts his personal experience in his book *Literacies of Power.* During his senior year, Macedo asked his guidance counselor for help with his college application. The guidance counselor promptly advised him to become a TV repairman. He explained to Macedo, "You have been in this country only two years, and you will never develop the necessary vocabulary to compete with the American-born who have been speaking English all their lives." Macedo was horrified and deflated. Luckily, he proved the counselor wrong. "What my guidance counselor failed to recognize," Macedo writes, "is that I was already fluent in three languages and that I had scored over 600 in both my Spanish and my French Achievement Tests. What my guidance counselor did was to equate my English-language development with my intellectual capacity." (6) There are countless similar stories around the country. This "linguistic chauvinism," (7) as UCLA Professor Otto Santa Ana describes in his book *Tongue-Tied*, often damages children's self-esteem and deflates their confidence; it judges them by how they speak English rather than by their intelligence and the content of what they are saying.

Unfortunately, when ESL students feel or hear negative judgments about themselves or their language skills, they start to believe that they're not good enough—that there's something wrong with them. This feeling of ignorance and inferiority can stay with children for many years. The intensity of their reactions will vary greatly, depending on other factors in their lives, of course. They might become depressed and feel alienated. They might suffer from a high level of anxiety, which can block learning. A common reaction is for children to want to break with their past completely and give up their native language in order to fit in.

The irony is that ESL students are actually ahead of the game and have several advantages over their classmates: They are learning to work with different cultural viewpoints, they are becoming more tolerant, *and* they already speak another language fluently! As one teacher, Mariana Souto-Manning, writes, "Instead of thinking of bilingualism as a malady that affects part of the population, against which teachers need to fight, we, educators and parents, need to start promoting bilingualism as augmenting and sophisticating children's thought processes, and serving as a resource for all children." (8)

My sister Marie-Eve was thirteen years old when we arrived in the U.S. She didn't speak any English, but she became a diligent student and went on to become a doctor with a specialty in tropical medicine. She worked internationally for many years and learned Portuguese, as well as some Arabic and Khmer for basic communication. She eventually joined the humanitarian organization Medecins Sans Frontieres (Doctors Without Borders). In 1999, MSF won the Nobel Peace Prize for its commitment in helping displaced populations around the world. On December 10th of that year, Marie-Eve took center stage in Oslo, Norway, and proudly accepted the Nobel Peace Prize on behalf of MSF. She was chosen because she represented the quintessential MSF worker. But, as Marie-Eve likes to point out, being fluent in several languages—and therefore capable of handling the countless interviews with international news agencies following the ceremony—didn't hurt either! When I think of her as a young ESL student who briefly was placed in special education classes, and compare that to what she has accomplished since in her medical career, the word "deficient" doesn't come to mind. In order to make the most out of the current ESL programs, it's important to remember that, as Professor Cummins writes, "Learning can be defined as the integration of new knowledge or skills with the knowledge or skills we already possess. It is crucial, therefore, to activate EL students' preexisting knowledge so that they can relate new information to what they already know." (9)

Unexpected Factors that Influence the Learning Curve

It's difficult to predict how well children will acquire a second language, considering the long list of unexpected factors that can influence their process. According to the research, we have to consider the child's aptitude for languages, his motivation, his personality, his level of self-esteem, the learning environment, his comfort level with the teacher's communication style, the context of the lessons, the status of his native language in his new community, and more. Even certain seemingly unrelated factors, such as the arrival of a new sibling or financial problems at home, will create stress and affect a child's learning curve as he tries to master a second language and adjust to a new environment.

Parents and teachers must avoid placing the child's budding bilingualism at the center of all the difficulties of adjusting to a new country. For example, if a Korean child is shy around playmates who speak only English, he will not necessarily become more outgoing if his exposure to Korean is reduced. As parents, we ask ourselves so many questions as we try to raise our children bilingually that it's easy to start doubting our choices or believing that any problem that emerges is directly related to our language choices.

In the U.S. we live in a society in which monolingualism is still the norm, and in which our information sources sometimes perpetuate myths and misconceptions about bilingualism that we constantly have to fight against. Professor Grosjean wrote in 1982, "It is difficult to forecast at this time whether this country will one day accept its cultural and linguistic diversity and whether the monolingual majority will finally realize that being bilingual and bicultural in the United States does not mean being "un-American." (10) This uncertainty still holds true today. But I believe we're at a turning point now, as more and more families hold on to their world languages and local, state, and federal organizations come together to support the economic, cultural, social, and cognitive benefits of learning more than one language.

Helping Our Children Integrate

If you look at the literature on children who move from one culture to another, you'll come across terms such as *global nomad, third-culture kid, army brat, missionary kid,* and *cross-cultural kid.* The identity development of a soon-to-be bicultural or multicultural child is complex and will continue to shape and reshape itself throughout her lifetime. Because crossing cultures is now so prevalent, it's becoming a major field of study, and you can find excellent books on the subject. (I posted a list of my personal recommendations on the website.) It's been fourteen years since my last cultural transition, and I'm still seeing the effects of a mobile childhood—from the obvious ones, such as writing this book and hoping to make a change in the way we raise and treat bilingual children, to the more obscure, like regularly moving furniture around my house when I haven't traveled for a while! (I'm not the only one, right?)

An important part of our children's integration into a new culture involves how we as parents adjust to our new surroundings. If we're conflicted all the time, how can we expect our children to see things clearly?

As we find ways to integrate our own identities, how do we help our children as they grow with multiple cultural influences? According to Dugan Romano, author of *Intercultural Marriage: Promises and Pitfalls*, "The secret appears to lie in the parents' ability to encourage open discussion of the children's mixed heritage, as well as the opportunity given the children to develop positive relationships with both cultural or racial groups." (11)

Let's look at the first part. Some parents wonder whether to emphasize or de-emphasize the family's complex mixed background to their children, but there is now overwhelming evidence that children do better—emotionally and academically—when they're encouraged to explore their cultural heritage. One eye-opening study looked at the well-being of Arab-European adolescents living in Israel. As researcher Hisham Motkal Abu-Rayya of Cambridge University noted, because these adolescents have to deal with enormous external tension, it's easy to assume that they would experience a confused sense of self and high levels of anxiety and tension over their mixed ethnic identity. Through his extensive and revealing questionnaires, Abu-Rayya concluded that adolescents who are active in their families' cultural traditions, have a clear way to identify themselves, and show pride in their heritage are happier and have a healthier sense of self. (12)

The second part of Romano's strategy involves helping our children fully participate in both their cultures. Many parents worry that their children will always feel that they are "in-between" rather than full participants in both cultures. But if we help them develop happy and positive relationships with relatives and young children their age from both cultural groups, they will have an easier time accessing all the benefits and resources of growing up bicultural.

My parents felt it was important never to criticize an American cultural trait or value in front of us, even as they dealt with a certain amount of culture shock themselves. "You have to keep a high level of enthusiasm and a desire to learn a new way of life," my mother says, "along with a good sense of humor of course when everything goes wrong!" (13) Neither of my parents compared the two cultures in terms of right and wrong, or better or worse; instead they focused on the experience itself as a way to explore a different vision of the world. If parents are curious and eager to explore their new surroundings, children will join in. We have to point out the similarities between our new home and where we used to live, and discover and adjust to the differences together. Harriet Cannon, a marriage and family therapist who specializes in multicultural relationships, has great advice that many parents need to hear. She writes, "The dominant culture of the country in which you now live will become your child's dominant cultural identity influence and there is no way to prevent it . . . . When you stay non-judgmental (and mean it) about the positive things in the dominant culture, you allow your child to be proud of his/her blend of culture by modeling it." (14) This is not always a given, but it's critical to our children's sense of well-being.

As our children learn to integrate different cultural values, beliefs, and assumptions, they naturally develop a broad definition of identity. They learn not to define themselves by a little box on a census form, but rather by the many layers they deem relevant. Even without a multicultural background, people usually identify themselves in many different ways, according to what they consider salient at that particular moment in their lives; their religion, perhaps, or their race, their education, their gender, their profession, their socioeconomic status, or their marital status. Ideally, our children will learn not to box people in and not impose limits on how others identify themselves.

It's naïve, however, to think that there is a specific timetable for raising happy, well-integrated bicultural children. Even as adults, when we think we have successfully integrated our different cultures, we'll experience events that will create unexpected, albeit temporary, chaos. The political situation in the U.S. at the beginning of the war in Iraq in 2003 was one such trigger for me—in particular, the deterioration in the relationship between the U.S. and France. I felt off balance when a series of books was published here by prominent authors with such titles as *How the French Betrayed America;*, *The French War Against America: How a Trusted Ally Betrayed Washington and the Founding Fathers;* and *Our Oldest Enemy: A History of America's Disastrous Relationship with France.* The animosity grew stronger as I experienced one particularly awkward and mean-spirited taxi ride on my way to the airport one morning, with the driver vehemently expressing his distaste for French people. It didn't help when the members of Congress actually took the time to organize a meeting to change the name French fries to "Freedom fries" on their cafeteria menu. This political tension, along with the feeling that I had to take sides, made me realize, once again, that our identity is fluid, that it keeps developing, that it's a life process, even when we think we have everything figured out!

Maintaining and Progressing in the First Language

During our first trip back to France and Belgium, two years after we permanently settled in New Jersey, my sisters and I spoke a mix of English and French, often in the same sentence. For my relatives back in France, self-declared language purists, this particular stage of our language development was unimpressive, to say the least. Adding English words in our speech was often interpreted as arrogant and condescending. If only I knew then what I know now about first-language attrition, I could have defended myself against the rolling eyes and whispers of "We've lost them."

Studies indicate that it's normal for the brain to "forget," or put aside, words in one language when we are learning a second language. It can be quite stressful, but the research shows that it's both temporary *and* necessary. According to University of Oregon psychologist Benjamin Levy and his colleague Dr. Michel Anderson, the brain adapts to learning a second language by temporarily setting aside the native language. (15)

In their research, Levy and Anderson found that during this particular period of language development, people do not simply forget words because of lack of practice. To learn a new expression in the second language inhibits the corresponding word in the native language, making it harder to remember later on. Their findings also showed that native language inhibition was present in the early stages of second-language acquisition and that fluent bilingual speakers were less affected. The process might seem frustrating at first, but we need to remember that this "forgetfulness" is temporary and allows the brain to absorb new knowledge. I vividly remember going through this process, although I didn't know what it was at the time. During my first year in the U.S., I struggled with simple French words and wondered how I could forget common expressions overnight when I had used them throughout my childhood.

One method for helping our children build on their first language skills is what Professor Stephen D. Krashen calls "de facto bilingual education." (16) A good bilingual education program, he explains, must include three elements: knowledge of the subject matter, literacy, and English-language development. If such a program is not available for your children in school, "de facto bilingual education" can happen at home.

For my sisters and me, our bilingual education happened around the dining room table. My parents would sit with us, and we would spend our evenings translating homework, discussing it in French, and translating our answers back in English. It might sound intimidating to some people, but it's all in the tone of the conversation. My parents found ways to keep it interesting for us. During these conversations, we connected as a family—an invaluable experience when life outside was confusing and difficult. My sisters and I were free to vent the frustrations and worries that come with culture shock; most importantly, we had our parents' full attention. As is the case with many families, the experience of learning a second language together can create a powerful alliance. It becomes an activity that bonds, like a good family game night, because it forces you to slow down, listen, and acknowledge one another. Children are naturally curious about the world around them, and if we can find ways, as parents, to tap into that creativity and enthusiasm, then the learning process can inspire and stimulate, even under the stress of an international relocation. In addition, when a child has access to books and reads regularly in both languages, he will pick up academic vocabulary and increase his chances of succeeding in school. It's important also to remember that only when students use both their languages systematically can they truly gain all the cultural, social, academic, and eventually economic benefits of being bilingual.

Researchers today recommend that parents and children discuss homework in both home and school languages.(17) A student who can process, analyze, and rephrase his school work in his home language, instead of just repeating it verbatim in the school language, will grasp it more fully. Also, discussing homework in two languages helps children learn specialized terminology in the heritage language—terminology that doesn't come up in regular family conversations. It's also a good exercise for all bilingual parents, helping us expand on our vocabulary in our native language. This form of bilingual education is, I believe, a crucial reason why my sisters and I became bilingual and biliterate.

Another way to help our children maintain their native language is to share cultural traditions together and hold on to our sense of ethnic pride. For some families, it means coming together during religious holidays or sharing a traditional meal. For other families, it can be an evening of oral storytelling with a grandfather or a trip to revisit important family sites. At our house growing up we often indulged in children's favorite French food, like Nutella on a piece of baguette in the morning or delicious crepes (paper thin pancakes.) A meal of crepes (with jam, Nutella, or fresh fruits) was sometimes all it took to bring back our pride in all things French. It was especially sweet to be allowed to eat them for dinner. My parents knew what they were doing! Chapter 9 will give you ideas for activities that can inspire your child's and your family's ethnic pride.

Peers

There comes a point in every child's life when he begins to expand his social circle, making friends in school and playgroups. He quickly figures out that people around him don't speak his two languages and that the dominant language seems the most effective. At this point, parents need to make an effort to include family and friends his age who share his heritage language, to show him that there's a need to speak that language as well. Research shows—and seasoned parents agree—that peers represent another critical component to successfully raising bilingual children.

Personal relationships provide a way for children to maintain and progress in their heritage language, but also bring a sense of pride in their cultural background. Children need confirmation from their peers that their native language is relevant. Our powers as parents fade somewhat when children develop their first friendships, and the opinions and preferences of peers start to play an important role in their decision-making.

A year or so after we settled in Westfield, New Jersey, my parents became friends with another French couple in a nearby town, who had two children close in age to my sisters and me. We often got together, and we became very close. I also became good friends with a new student in my 9th grade class who had just relocated from France. These friendships made me want to continue speaking French. I liked the idea that with two languages I could cast a larger net and communicate with more people, and make more friends than I would if I only spoke one language. At that age, it also became a fun way for my French friends and me to differentiate ourselves from the pack, or to say things we didn't want other people to understand!

My sisters and I were also fortunate to bond with several groups of French-speaking exchange students throughout high school. I remember the pride I felt in being able to speak French fluently with them. One group happened to become very popular with the other American students in our school, especially the good-looking French boys, which made it even sweeter to take center stage with them for those few weeks. I became fast friends with them, as it often happens when you meet someone in a foreign land who speaks your native language. We bonded like long-lost cousins. I felt happy and relieved to be around kids who acted the same way I did. I understood all the cultural markers, but at the same time I found myself opening their minds about what life was like in the U.S.

Another resource for meeting students who speak the same native language is, of course, the Internet. Technological advances such as webcams and free online telephone services can serve as a vital social support for children to stay in touch with friends back home or meet new ones. Parents can also use helpful language groups and social networks online to connect with other families who are trying to raise bilingual children. If children feel like they're the ones making a choice to speak their native language, by building friendships locally or online, they will be motivated to keep up their language skills.

Working Together

Positive integration into a new culture requires a great deal of work and open communication between parents and children. Even if children seem to be adjusting well, they're going to experience a lot of stress and ambiguity, and you need to keep a watchful eye on them. Parents who've weathered the storm seem to agree that maintaining a healthy relationship between parent and child is half the battle!

Many of us expect our children to stay connected to their language and ethnic culture and, at the same time, integrate and excel in the community language in order to be successful. It's feasible, as millions of bilingual and bicultural professionals can attest, but families have to work at it. For example, parents need to show interest and enthusiasm toward their new environment. They can promote all the qualities of the new culture, they can see the sights locally and across the country, they can read travel guides, and they can participate in family-oriented community events. Parents can read every day with their children in their native language and find books that focus on their children's individual interests and hobbies. Grandparents can share stories of their native country and explain the similarities and differences with the U.S. culture. The whole family can work together to learn English.

As I'll discuss in Chapter 4, we now have extensive research at our fingertips and can take concrete steps to help our children successfully integrate their rich linguistic and cultural backgrounds. There may be some dark moments in a family's adjustment to a new culture, but they're often temporary, and the rewards of being bilingual and bicultural will eventually spill into all facets of life. I hope you're finding, in this book, the tools you need to make informed language decisions for your family to help you raise the next generation of well-educated, globally-minded citizens.

CHAPTER 4

Challenges at Home

Nobody trips over mountains. It is the small pebble that causes you to stumble. Pass all the pebbles in your path, and you will find you have crossed the mountain.

Author Unknown

When Cultures Collide

Raising children often puts our own upbringing under a microscope. We reflect on our families' values and beliefs, how we define ourselves, and what we want to pass on to our children. For international couples, there are a lot of pieces to bring together! At the heart of many of our arguments lies a subtle cultural misunderstanding. The reality is that when we're fighting over Amy's lack of progress in Korean or Emanuel's tendency to mix his two languages, there are often deeper issues at play.

It's helpful to start by identifying the values we've internalized since childhood. If we become aware of our values, beliefs, and assumptions and how they translate into our particular style of parenting, then we may have an easier time raising bilingual and bicultural children together.

In his world-renowned research, Dutch anthropologist Geert Hoefstede came up with four helpful "cultural dimensions" and classified countries under each one. (1) Although the study was initially done to explain how culture affects the relationships between international business corporations, it also applies well to families' relationships. Hoefstede's research is powerful; I predict that it will raise your level of awareness every time you interact with someone from a different cultural background. As with any cross-cultural research, these value dimensions represent only generalizations, but they will help us identify how our values influence our everyday behavior and may help bring about cultural awareness to help us bridge those differences.

INDIVIDUALISM	COLLECTIVISM
Focus is on personal needs and goals	Strong ties to the family, promoting interdependence. Caring for one another comes before personal needs.
Children are taught to speak up	Children are taught to listen
• United States	• Venezuela
• Australia	• Pakistan
• Netherlands	• Taiwan
• New Zealand	• Chile

This cultural orientation reveals itself during disagreements, for example, on whether to let the child sleep in his own crib or in the parents' bedroom; or whether to teach the child to self-soothe by letting him cry for a while or pick him up right away to comfort him. A parent from an individualistic culture often prefers to teach his children to be self-sufficient early on. As soon as a young child can hold a spoon or a cup in his hand, he is taught to eat and drink on his own. A parent from a collectivistic culture might assist her child longer and delay using a drinking cup. Author Alberto Fantini relates a revealing anecdote about this cultural difference in his book *Language Acquisition of a Bilingual Child*. His case study was a 5-year-old boy named Mario, who was teased all the time by his friends and relatives for drinking his milk from a baby bottle. Having been raised by multicultural parents, however, Mario would never try to hide his bottle. On the contrary, he usually held it up with great pride. Fantini writes, "He knew that in some places at least, like Bolivia and Mexico, (where his mom had grown up) drinking from a "mamadera" was perfectly acceptable behavior, even for children his age." (2)

In a collectivistic culture many people believe that as a child grows older, he has a stronger obligation to consider the consequences of his actions on others. For example, if a teenager in the U.S. doesn't do well in school, it's mostly a reflection on his own skills and abilities, whereas in a collectivistic culture such as Japan, his poor performance reflects on the whole family, and the situation brings shame to the group.

SMALL-DISTANCE POWER	LARGE-DISTANCE POWER
Equality between family members.	Parental and grandparental authority over children is seldom questioned.
Informal approach	Formal approach
• Austria	• Mexico
• Israel	• India
• Ireland	• Singapore
• Sweden	• Brazil

In large-distance power cultures, there is an emphasis on formality. For example, in France, children learn early on to use the *vous* form, or the *you* plural, to address elders. As they grow, they learn to use it when addressing people of a higher status or people they meet for the first time. Siblings also each have a rank in the family, which grants them different discretions.

Friction can occur between parents who were raised on opposite sides of this cultural orientation. One parent may expect complete authority when making decisions for the family; the other parent may prefer to give the children more power and engage them in the decision process.

My husband and I noticed our cultural differences in the way we let children interrupt adult conversations. In large-distance power cultures such as France, children are often taught to wait for adults to finish talking, whereas in small-distance power cultures, children's needs often come first, and parents will break a conversation to attend to them. In some families, this informality can be misinterpreted as a lack of respect for the elders.

WEAK UNCERTAINTY AVOIDANCE	STRONG UNCERTAINTY AVOIDANCE
Children learn from taking risks and are encouraged to ask questions	Children are guided along a path, and deviation is not encouraged.
Change is good	Set rules and regulations
• Singapore	• Greece
• Sweden	• Portugal
• South Africa	• Belgium
• Australia	• Japan

The third cultural dimension affects the way parents control their children. Parents who come from a strong uncertainty-avoidance culture often impose more restrictions on their children when it comes to activities such as spending time after school with friends or attending parties in the evening. Such parents may not be comfortable letting go of their authority and discipline, and thus they might refuse to send their children to summer camps or on faraway field trips.

In the U.S., where most parents have a weak uncertainty orientation, children are given more freedom and flexibility in their choices. Public schools, for example, offer an amazing range of classes that encourage new and diverse ideas. Children can study journalism or woodworking or music. In a strong uncertainty culture, the school's curriculum is often more predictable and doesn't encourage different ways of thinking.

MASCULINITY	FEMININITY
Dominant values geared toward assertiveness and the acquisition of things.	Dominant values geared toward a genuine concern for people and their quality of life.
• Venezuela	• Sweden
• Italy	• Chile
• Philippines	• France
• Columbia	• Turkey

The fourth cultural dimension affects parents' expectations about how their children should be socialized. In "masculine" cultures, a boy is expected to be tough and success-driven. A girl, on the other hand, is expected to be discreet and focused on family issues. Disagreements caused by this cultural orientation can show up in unexpected ways. For example, if one parent is from a masculine culture, where achievement and ambition are important, and the other parent is from a feminine culture, where rich and nurturing family time comes first, discussions about how much children should get involved with after-school activities quickly becomes complicated.

Different cultural values and beliefs do not have to be a constant source of tension and frustration. Once we clarify our own values, attitudes, behavior patterns, and goals as a family, we can develop strategies to deal with our disagreements. We can use our differences to teach our children early on that there is more than one way to look at things.

When children witness cooperation in their own home, they learn that people can have different perspectives on issues but still respect one another. We are their first role models to show that contradictory ways of thinking do not have to lead to fighting; they can engender mutual respect and compromises.

One Syrian and American couple aptly describes their hope, shared by many parents raising bilingual children:

> "Our goal is to have them feel like natives in both countries—to be able to speak Arabic and English; to feel comfortable kissing cheeks when greeting their Syrian relatives and hugging their American ones; to enjoy hamburgers and falafels; and to appreciate Beethoven, the Beatles, and Um Khartoum, the most famous singer of the Arabic-speaking world. We want them to have the security their Syrian cousins feel of being a part of a big clan in which all joys and sorrows are shared. At the same time, we hope they learn the lessons passed down from the American frontier; that they are free to pursue their individual dreams and have personal responsibility for what they make of themselves." (3)

All in the Family

RELUCTANT RELATIVES

In a perfect world, our in-laws would cheer us on as we attempt to do the very best for our children. But when a young child speaks a different language and absorbs different cultural behaviors and assumptions, grandparents sometimes struggle to adjust to the unknown. Part of it is simply human nature. We want to see ourselves in our children and grandchildren. Even parents of adopted children will often look for similarities in personality traits or physical features in their children to deepen the existing bond.

As I mentioned earlier, sometimes the tension between family members is linked to cultural differences. It helps to step back and try to understand where everyone's coming from. Literally. As we witness every day on the news, international cooperation is difficult and usually requires tact and diplomacy. Sometimes the tension is linked to issues that monolingual families face as well, such as personality traits, self-esteem, power, or simply personal preferences. For example, Sarah, a young mom from the Netherlands, believes her American mother-in-law just likes to feel included in the family's decisions; when she isn't, she often reacts with criticism, whether it's about her grandson's lack of progress in English or the clutter around the house. "She always finds something to pick on!" Sarah writes. "We just never let her attitude affect our commitment to raise our son with two languages because we know her complaints are not really about that." (4) Parents often find it worthwhile to sit down with close relatives and explain clearly why it's important for them to raise their children with two languages, the benefits of bilingualism, and how the family can support them.

Grandparents sometimes resist the idea of raising bilingual grandchildren, for a variety of reasons. For some grandparents, the concern is that speaking the minority language at home will make it impossible for the children to master English and excel in school. For others, especially if they're monolinguals, the fear is that the children will be overwhelmed and consequently not learn either language fluently. These grandparents may have struggled as adults to learn another language, so they believe their grandchildren's experience will be similar. Because of their cultural background, some grandparents may also find it awkward to come face-to-face with a four-year-old who has stronger language skills than they, the respected elders, do. These situations need to be handled with tact and compassion.

However well-meaning and heartfelt these grandparental concerns may be, research findings indicate that more damage will be done emotionally and intellectually if a child is cut off from his heritage language and culture. It's rarely in the child's best interest to stop speaking a parent's native language and possibly lose contact with one side of the family. Under normal circumstances, with motivation and support, children can learn any language they need to communicate. They will learn by playing, listening, and repeating, without worrying about pronunciation or dissecting grammar structures.

What can parents do when grandparents are concerned about their grandchildren being raised in two languages? First, we have to remind ourselves that we can't control other people's reactions and emotions toward bilingualism. Then we can provide reluctant relatives with well-researched studies that pertain to their specific fears and concerns; these studies may help them see a different perspective. We can also explain to them what bilingualism means to us, why it's important to our cultural identity, and why we believe that speaking two languages will ultimately be an important asset to our children.

Grandparents who speak the heritage language can play a pivotal role in motivating children to keep using it. Studies show that a strong relationship between grandparents and grandchildren can greatly influence the children's outlook on and maintenance of their heritage language, especially when they lack direct hands-on cultural experience Grandparents can share knowledge of their ethnic culture and can provide personal reflections and anecdotes about life in their native country. They can share family recipes and captivating stories to keep their grandchildren engaged. Today, my parents are using the same techniques they used with my sisters and me to keep their grandchildren interested in all things French. Their top priority when they pack their suitcases to visit us is to leave enough room for French books. We let them know about the girls' current interests, what they're curious about, and their vocabulary level, and they try to choose books accordingly. When we're not reading, we're usually planning our next meal! Considering how many of us fondly remember our grandmothers or mothers' cooking, we shouldn't underestimate the power of homemade meals to solidify our children's ethnic identity!

It's worth the effort to get grandparents and extended family on board because they all have the power to contribute something to our children's bilingual journey, whether or not they speak the heritage language. They can regularly praise the child's budding bilingualism; they can expose the social and economic benefits of knowing two languages; they can read and write to them in their heritage language; and they can even express their own frustrations at not speaking a second language as adults.

SPOUSAL SUPPORT

Sometimes the "reluctant relative" is our own partner. I met a woman at a playground who admitted with great sadness that her husband, who spoke fluent Tagalog, didn't feel compelled to speak it to their daughter. She said that everyone on his side of the family spoke fluent English; now that they lived in the U.S., they considered Tagalog a non-essential language. If your partner looks down on his or her own native language or does not see the benefits of teaching it to your child, you can share your personal motivations for wanting to raise a bilingual child and provide well-researched findings that point out the social, economic, and cultural benefits to speaking two languages. You can find books, children's songs, and interactive toys in your partner's language to use with your child when you're all together. Most importantly, you can study your partner's native language yourself to show your enthusiasm and your commitment.

If your partner speaks the majority language and looks down on *your* native language, it will also be challenging to raise a bilingual child. Children pick up on the lack of respect and low status of a heritage language very quickly, whether at home or in the community. As one Jordanian friend noted, "My husband doesn't speak Arabic and has never expressed an interest in learning it, so I never insisted on speaking it with our daughter. I didn't want my husband to feel excluded from our conversations." (5) If it's important to you to share your native language with your child, you still have the option to speak it when you're alone with her and share the majority language when the family is all together. It's a difficult way to become bilingual because it doesn't provide as much exposure to the minority language, but you'll cherish those private moments with your child. It's also important to remember that any amount of heritage language learning is positive as it can eventually help your child learn it more easily later on as an adult, if she chooses to.

An open-minded and supportive partner who doesn't speak your native language will see this as an opportunity to learn it along with your child. Your partner's respect and enthusiasm for your native language will have a direct effect on your child's willingness to learn it as well. However, parents who choose to learn a new language have to be ready for the occasional tease by their growing children when it comes to their mispronunciations or heavy accent! They might also be told—gently or otherwise—to refrain from using their second (or third) language in public during their children's sensitive school years. But it also gives parents the chance to turn the table and praise their children on their enviable bilingual skills. If handled with tact and empathy, learning a second language can be a fun way to connect and bring a family closer together.

SIBLING ISSUES

Siblings will choose to speak to one another in the language that feels most natural. For some young global nomads who relocate a few times during the course of their childhood, the chosen language might change to match the language of their local peers. For those of us who spoke only one language for many years before learning a second one, an emotional bond is often created in our native language that is difficult to change. As adults, my sisters and I rarely speak English to one another. In high school we did mix our two languages quite a bit and developed a preference for many English expressions that didn't have a French equivalent in our vocabulary. Now that we live in three different language environments (France, Cambodia, and the U.S.), we speak only French to one another.

Siblings who are raised with two languages from birth will often choose the dominant language early on. If parents wish to gently redirect them, they are usually more successful when they take the time to clearly explain to their children what it means to them to hear them speak their native language. Ultimately though, parents will have to accept the language their children choose to communicate with one another.

For now, Natasha and Sofiya use mostly English with one another. If I join in, they'll switch to French to address me but go back to English with each other. If I start a game with them in French—playing with their train set, for example—and I walk away, they'll promptly switch to English. The fascinating thing is that this occurs even during the weeks when I'm alone with them, during which their home environment is almost 100 percent French. (My husband has a seven-days-on, seven-days-off schedule, so every other week I'm alone with the girls.) We read, cook, eat, play, do crafts, cuddle, and watch DVDs, all in French. (Except for *Thomas the Tank Engine* films, which I haven't been able to find in French!) This development is a great testament, I believe, to the power of the dominant language and how quickly children understand its central role in their lives. It does not, however, indicate that they are losing their heritage language skills. Research shows that even though children choose to speak the dominant language with one another, it does not mean that they are not developing fluency in the heritage language as well.

Personally I don't try to redirect Natasha and Sofiya to speak French to one another because it doesn't feel natural. They were born in the U.S., and unless our situation changes, English will be their dominant language. But I will never stop speaking French to them.

Siblings of different ages sometimes show a dramatic difference in heritage language skills, which usually signals a decline in language exposure at home. Parents are often diligent with their firstborn and give them undivided attention and consistent native language input the first few years. Two different scenarios can happen with the birth of a second or third child. The older sibling will want to teach and use the minority language with the younger sibling to set a positive example. Or he will turn to the dominant language with the friendships he makes in preschool or kindergarten, the movies he watches, the books he reads, and the younger sibling will naturally turn to English as the preferred language. Other factors including a child's aptitude for languages, her personality, her one-on-one time with her parents, and their commitment to speaking their native language at home, will also influence the uneven level between siblings.

With a growing family parents soon break the cozy native language bubble they created at home those first few years with their first child. But we then have a choice to make. We can slowly give up using our native language, and let English take over our dinner conversations, or we can get creative and find fun and engaging activities to keep our language alive on a daily basis. There is no reason why passing on our native language should feel like homework, or only be used when we're disciplining our children, when we can play and have fun instead! We need to continue to speak our native language with our children, or else the critical element—the *need* to speak it—will be gone. Chapters 9 and 10 will give you a head start with 100 activities to do at home and in the community to help you keep your children bilingual. You can't control the language your children will use to speak to one another, but you can control the amount of exposure they receive in your native language by providing fun ways to speak it together!

TWINS

When it comes to raising bilingual twins, language development issues veer to specific circumstances like parent-child eye contact, twin language, and three-way conversations. (6) During the critical early years, parents of multiples often find it difficult to speak to each infant separately with prolonged eye contact, which is fundamental to a child's language development. In addition, a parent who cares for infant twins often engages in three-way communication except perhaps during baths and diaper changes. These specific environmental factors, as well as biological issues like low birth weight and premature birth, all have to be taken into consideration when examining language development issues, including language delay, in twins or triplets. It's important to remember that the average birth weight for a singleton is seven pounds seven ounces, whereas for a twin it's five pounds five ounces, according to the National Organization of Mothers of Twins Clubs. Also, almost half of all multiple births are premature. (7)

When parents are aware of these special circumstances that affect their children's language development, they can be reassured that any language issues that develop are not caused by the exposure to two languages but by other factors. They can then adjust the quality and quantity of their speech. Constant talking and engaging our children individually as much as possible from day one become crucial elements. If you have a particularly talkative relative or friend who speaks your native language, now's the time to invite her for dinner! We need to saturate their environment with a rich and varied vocabulary, focus on making eye contact with each child as we speak, and balance two-way conversations throughout the day, instead of speaking to both of them simultaneously.

As any parent of multiples will tell you, it's a challenge to monitor our activities in such a way. Most of the time we're just in survival mode! When Natasha and Sofiya were younger, I usually looked for ways to meets their needs simultaneously so that I could find pockets of time here and there to myself to recharge my batteries. Nonetheless, we need to be aware that raising twins creates a unique linguistic environment and that we need to make an extra effort to increase their daily exposure to their two languages. Small changes can make a big difference. For example, instead of addressing both children simultaneously with one command—"Let's clean up the toys!"—try to address each child individually. For example, "Sofiya, can you put your train cars in this basket?" and "Natasha, let's line up your teddy bears in this corner."

As with any challenge, it's helpful to keep some positives in mind for motivation. For example, research shows that twins learn to use the pronoun "I" faster than singletons. (8) They want to quickly stand out on their own! They also have a constant companion to engage in a dialogue with, which can trigger new vocabulary and sentence structures. They play games where they repeat each other's words, they learn from one another, and they may even correct each other's language mistakes.

One strategy that my husband, Vern, and I use today is to organize activities separately; we each spend individual time with Natasha or Sofiya—whether it's reading, playing, or taking a small trip together. We focus on eye contact as we talk to them, and we pay attention to their individual learning style. We narrate everything we do together and repeat vocabulary words they're learning or expressions they're struggling with. Since one of our daughters is more introverted than the other, this one-on-one time is valuable to give her a chance to express herself fully without her sister finishing her sentences! Vern and I tell ourselves we're doing this for their language development, but secretly it feels like a mini-vacation for us to only have to take care of one child at a time!

Setbacks

LIMITED VOCABULARY

One of my personal challenges in this journey of raising bilingual children is to improve my French vocabulary as the girls get older. Because I left France at age twelve, I never acquired extensive vocabulary in fields such as science and technology. I want to be able to discuss diverse subjects without always taking out my dictionary! Even today, Natasha and Sofiya will reach for it on the bookshelf when they hear me struggling to find a word. (It could be a sign of aging, too!) "Wheelbarrow . . . wheelbarrow, what's the word for wheelbarrow?" Or better yet, one of them will look at me and say, "*Brouette*, Maman!" Which is always a great reminder to never underestimate our children's capacity for learning.

The solution to a limited vocabulary is, of course, to read more in our native language, whatever the reading material—magazines, books, or articles online. It also helps to write letters or emails to friends and family members. For many of us who left our native country at an early age, having children and deciding to raise them in our native language gives us a chance to become students again and learn our language more thoroughly. I like to think that it also makes our children realize how important languages are to us and how beneficial it is to perfect them, at any age.

It's common for immigrants and global nomads to have vocabulary gaps and grammatical difficulties in their native languages, especially if they didn't have access to bilingual education programs in school. It takes effort and commitment to develop our language skills. For children to become fluent in two languages, their language exposure has to include learning opportunities outside the home to build a more academic vocabulary. We'll look at schooling options in Chapter 5 as a way to increase their language input.

ISOLATION

The Modern Language Association has a fantastic tool on its website that lets you find out how many speakers of other world languages live in your community. Needless to say, parents who are raising bilingual children in New York, for example, might not find a sympathetic ear from parents in Pierre, South Dakota, when they start complaining about isolation! For families who live in seemingly monolingual communities, it's often a surprise to see how many international languages are spoken behind closed doors by your neighbors. According to the MLA website, in my zip code there are more than 1,300 people who speak a language besides English, including more than 300 who speak French. (9) Once you find out you're not alone, you can start reaching out by organizing a bilingual or multilingual playgroup with other families in your community. It's not difficult to get started—as you'll see in Chapter 10—and it offers all the elements to promote heritage language maintenance.

If you live in Maine, for example, and you speak Vietnamese with your child, chances are you're feeling pretty isolated. According to the MLA map, there are only 93 Vietnamese speakers in your state! It's a difficult obstacle to overcome, but don't give up! More and more parents use the Internet to fight isolation. A DSL connection and a webcam can go a long way to develop ties with other children who are learning the same heritage language. Trips to your native country, when financially possible, are also a great way to immerse your child in his heritage language and give him firsthand experience in your cultural traditions. After a successful trip, your child can stay in touch with his cousins and friends and keep up his language skills by communicating online, "face-to-face," with a webcam. I hope the list of activities in Chapters 9 and 10 will inspire you to keep speaking your native language and engage your children in fun and creative ways.

DIVORCE

This is a complicated issue with many layers, and the experience is unique to each family member going through it. In most cases, parents will have to reevaluate how much time the children will be exposed to the minority language and reassess their goals. If the child will have continued interactions with both sides of the family, there can still be a thread of continuity in both languages that can help the child with one less disruption. Also, the linguistic environment might actually become less mixed, and therefore give the child a better chance to become fluent in both languages. The need to speak the native language on each side of the family will be more pronounced.

If the ties with one side of the family are completely severed, however, and the remaining parent doesn't speak the minority language, it's clear that the child's motivation to learn it will be nonexistent for the time being. But later on, as the child becomes a young adult, there might be another opportunity to relearn the language to get a better understanding of his linguistic and cultural heritage. As many adult bilinguals have experienced, bilingualism comes in waves, and one language can reappear after years of not speaking it. The need and the motivation to speak a particular language remain key factors in becoming bilingual.

RELOCATION

In 2006, there were more than 38,000,000 foreign-born individuals living in the U.S., up from 31,000,000 in 2000, according to the Migration Policy Institute. (10) For parents who are raising children in two languages, a relocation can complicate the family's language plan. Parents can choose to keep speaking their native language with their children and let the new school environment and the community introduce the new language. Parents learn the new language along with their children and make it a family affair, without breaking the emotional bond that was created with their children's first languages.

When parents decide to switch languages, it has to be handled with care and thoughtful consideration. Most researchers agree that with young children, a change in the family's language system can be risky. Research shows that children under age six are especially vulnerable emotionally if they suddenly have to communicate with one parent in a different language. (11) When faced with these difficult decisions, it's important to remember the link between language and culture. Parents are not just switching languages with their children. Even at a young age, a child's languages are linked to his cultural identity, and suddenly discarding one can have serious ramifications. Parents might also expose different personality traits depending on which language they speak, which can be confusing to a young child. They might become more assertive or less confident depending on the language. I consider myself more extroverted in French than in English. I also become more animated and speak louder in French, according to my husband! All these factors can affect a child's emotional reaction to a change in languages in the home. As Professor Genesee reminds us, "Young children often react badly to inconsistent or irregular exposure to language; they like consistency. Thus, if parents decide to raise their child bilingual, they should do so only if they can provide continuous and extended exposure to both languages . . . . Children need long term exposure to language if they are to develop full competence." (12)

After a relocation, some parents drop their native language and let the dominant language take over because they worry that their child will not otherwise have enough opportunities to learn the new language. However, the community language is rarely the one to suffer. The motivation to learn is high and there are countless opportunities for children to pick it up everywhere they go, from peers, teachers, in town, the movies, billboards, magazines, television, video games, et cetera. Their new language is all around them. Parents who continue to speak their native language, on the other hand, provide a crucial "thread of continuity" that can ease the transition to a new cultural environment for their children. It becomes one less challenge for them to overcome. They also lead their children toward a more positive sense of self, a stronger education, a well-integrated identity, and more job opportunities in the future.

Creating a Bilingual Home

PROVIDE EXPOSURE TO THE HERITAGE LANGUAGE

Very often I encounter parents who are disappointed that their children are not bilingual but who also readily admit that they themselves speak English to their children more than their native language. If that's the case, the child has rightfully concluded that if her parents don't speak their native language, she doesn't have to either! The first thing we need to do is to keep speaking our languages daily, not just for a few private cuddle moments or during scolding sessions, but during fun and varied activities and outings to broaden our children's vocabulary. We also need to expand our support network and find friends and relatives who can speak our native language with our children. They will help demonstrate the need for this second language. The 100 activities detailed in Chapters 9 and 10 are part of the solution as we try to keep our world languages vital and relevant. We need to get creative to make sure we incorporate our languages in our daily lives in the most natural and engaging ways. As Traute Taeschner, author of *The Sun is Feminine*, points out, "Not all children who grow up in bilingual families become bilingual . . . . The undeniable need to communicate is sufficient motivation to make the child speak one or more languages, but it is also absolutely indispensable." (13)

Although many of us hope our children will express themselves well in both languages, there are unquestionable benefits to any degree of language exposure we can give them. Don't give up, even if you're only using your native language sporadically. Your circumstances or your motivation might change over time. Even passive learning of a language has positive consequences. For example, some students report the ability to remember their native language later on in college while studying it as a foreign language, while others discover a talent in learning languages in general. Let's hope that this book inspires you to start speaking your native language more often, enabling you to become more connected to your cultural heritage and pass on to your children all the extraordinary benefits of speaking a second language.

MAKE THE HERITAGE LANGUAGE RELEVANT

For some parents, the challenge is not finding the motivation to speak their native language every day, but convincing their children to do so as well. Parents are often surprised when a child rejects their native language. We take it personally, and it stings. Although it is usually a temporary phase, it can turn language learning into a struggle or an emotional roller-coaster. As one mom writes, "I am tired of insisting that my daughter speak only Russian with me. She is 10 now, and as she gets older, it's getting worse and worse. My husband is American. She is telling him everything, communicating with him in English, and I feel terrible and isolated." (14) It's true that children quickly understand which language holds a higher status in the community, which language is spoken by the majority, and which language is more effective in their everyday lives. So what can a parent do when a child understands two languages but starts to only speak one? Regardless of what strategy you use, you have a better chance at succeeding if you keep it lighthearted, tactful, and nonthreatening.

Your child will choose the language he wants to express himself in, but you can increase the importance of your native language as a way to make it as appealing and effective as the dominant language. It's important for children at this stage to meet other people, especially peers, who speak the same language. One parent found great success by inviting a favorite cousin to stay with them for the summer holidays. Another parent, a Canadian living in the U.S., collected all the information she could find in French on her son's favorite sport, hockey, and took him to local games, on the condition that he speak French the whole time. This stage requires parents to make an extra effort and create an environment in which the language has a prominent place in the family's daily life in *and* outside the home. The activities in Chapters 9 and 10 will help you jumpstart the process.

EXPLAIN THE BENEFITS

A child needs to be reminded of the many cultural, social, educational, and eventually economic benefits of speaking two languages and understanding the cultural nuances of two countries. For preschoolers like Natasha and Sofiya, it means being reminded of how great it is to be able to speak with their seven first cousins on Skype, sing songs together, and watch T'choupi (a French cartoon character) on YouTube. For older children, it means being reminded that they can join or even become president of the German club in school, read German comic books, or choose a penpal who speaks the same language. My parents made it clear to my sisters and me that bilingualism opens doors. Some parents have also reported success by asking other family members or friends to endorse bilingualism in front of the children and remind them how much easier it is to learn a language at a young age. They can also drop names of famous actors, singers, or athletes who speak the same native language. (I've included a list on the website for this book at www.bilingualbychoice.com)

STRENGTHEN THEIR VOCABULARY

Refusing to speak the heritage language sometimes signals that the child does not feel comfortable expressing herself in that language yet because she lacks the proper vocabulary. If this is the case, it's important to give her opportunities to hear and interact in the heritage language to build up her confidence and self-esteem and strengthen her vocabulary. It's important to remember that she's not rejecting the language as much as she's letting you know that she doesn't feel confident that she can speak it well. Encouragement, patience, and praising every little step are key ingredients at this stage. You can use the 50 activities in Chapter 9 to guide you through this process.

KEEP THE CONVERSATION GOING

Let's look at the different strategies parents have developed to keep the conversation going when their child starts to express himself only in the dominant language.

1. "I pretend I don't understand."

When a child inadvertently uses the dominant language, parents can reply in the native language by saying "I didn't understand. What did you say?" to guide them back. The consensus on this strategy is that it can only done in a playful and tactful way, and probably not continuously. It breaks the rhythm of the conversation and can frustrate a child as he tries to tell a story or share his feelings. In addition, this strategy can backfire if the child decides it's easier to engage the other parent instead. Parents can make it work if they keep it light and turn it into a game, especially with young children. One couple reported having great success with this method after they took the time to explain to their children how much it meant to hear them speak in the heritage language. The gentle nudge in pretending not to understand was enough to remind their children to pay attention to what they saying. Kindness and humor will go a long way in raising bilingual children!

2. "I ask my child to repeat in the heritage language."

Another common approach by parents is to gently sway them back to the heritage language with a kind request. *"En Espanol, por favor!"* can be repeated regularly, in the same way we have to repeat "Brush your teeth!" every night. Parents shouldn't feel bad about having to redirect children; it's just part of parenting and knowing what's ultimately best for our children, until they realize it themselves one day and say "thank you!" You should never feel guilty when you're trying to raise bilingual children, just as you would never feel guilty about pressing them over and over again to say please and thank you.

Parents can usually quickly determine, based on their child's mood, whether to pursue the request to switch languages. The context of the situation plays an important role. As Taeschner points out, "When a child comes home from school and is excited to relate a story, it's best to let him use the language it happened in." (15) If a child is frustrated or angry and in need of immediate attention, it's best to worry less about proper language use and attend to the child's emotions instead. When a child is calm and content and not feeling rushed, the request to switch languages will obviously be much better received. Always asking a child to switch languages is potentially damaging. As Taeschner points out, "With time, it becomes harder and harder for the adult to interrupt speech continually, doubling the amount of time needed for each interaction. In the long run, this request is accompanied by anxiety, unhappiness, and dissatisfaction, culminating in an overall state of frustration, and the parent feels he has failed in bringing up his child as a bilingual." (16)

Parents who have successfully overcome this obstacle report that children's rejection of the home language is usually temporary. Parents need to continue to speak their native language even if the child's response is not always enthusiastic. As one parent writes, "Do not let the children dissuade you from speaking your own language to them, and don't put a time frame on anything—they'll absorb both languages in their own time and way." (16)

3. *"I repeat in my native language what my child has just said."*

Parents sometimes repeat what their child has just said, but in the form of a question, and then they answer the question. "You want to go play in the snow? You have to put your boots on first. You don't know where they are? Take a look in the closet, and I will help you put them on." When Natasha and Sofiya speak English to me, which is not very often at this point, this method feels the most natural to me. I do it without even thinking about it. The result is that I keep speaking French to them, and it subconsciously sways them back to French as well. I also choose this way of keeping the conversation flowing because it keeps me from having to correct them all the time.

Seasoned parents also recommend stepping up the exposure to the minority language at this stage in fun and thoughtful ways geared toward the child's interests. A variety of engaging activities, both in and outside the home confirms to children that their heritage language is relevant, indispensable, and effective in their daily conversations. It creates deep and enduring family ties and connections with peers who share the same language. It helps them develop a richer and more academic vocabulary and brings them one step closer to becoming bilingual.

CHAPTER 5

Schooling Options

My parents told me, "Finish your dinner. People in China and India are starving." I tell my daughters, "Finish your homework. People in India and China are starving for your job."

Author Thomas L. Friedman

Homeschooling

To raise their children to read and write in two languages and acquire academic vocabulary in the minority language, more and more parents are choosing to educate them at home. Close to 1.5 million children were homeschooled in the U.S. in 2007, which represents a remarkable 74 percent increase since 1999. About 15 percent of these homeschooled children are minorities. (1)

Although early advocates of homeschooling chose it to reinforce religious teachings, today families choose it for a variety of reasons. Some families choose it because they are dissatisfied with public schools. They may not approve of the environment; they may prefer a more individualistic or nontraditional approach to education; they may want more flexibility for their children's sports training; or they may have children with special needs. As my husband recently noted, homeschooling can also be a great option when parents decide to sell their house, live on a boat, and sail the world with their children! Today, homeschooling is taking place in many different neighborhoods, across all socioeconomic groups.

Homeschooling demands discipline, commitment, and sacrifice—and the results are impressive. Homeschooled students do as well as—and sometimes better than—students in the public school system. According to Lindsey M. Burke at the Heritage Foundation in Washington, D.C., "Homeschooled students succeed academically regardless of family income or teacher certification of parents. Top-tier colleges and universities also recognize the academic abilities of homeschooled students, with Stanford, Yale, and Harvard among the institutions with the most homeschool-friendly policies." (2) Because homeschooling as an educational option continues to grow, families can find numerous organizations that will help them prepare a plan of action, locate appropriate curriculum, and take the time to answer all of their questions and concerns.

More often than not, homeschooling families are single-income families, but generally both parents contribute their time and personal strengths, especially if they each speak a different language. For Corey Heller, the editor-in-chief of *Multilingual Living* magazine, homeschooling her three children involved researching and studying the schools curriculum from both Germany and the U.S. But she also enjoys keeping the lessons flexible and focusing on what her children are interested in. She writes, "We allow ourselves to pick and choose what we want to cover when and we are definitely advocates of letting our children learn at their own pace. It just so happens that our five-year-old can read well in both languages, but that doesn't mean our other children will learn to read by age five—and that is just fine with us!"

Parents who are considering homeschooling might worry about the seeming lack of socialization. According to Heller, this misconception is widespread. She writes, "Homeschooling is actually an extremely social form of education . . . . In fact, our local homeschooling group in Seattle has more than 200 families who organize activities almost every day of the week." (3)

For Helene Alvarez, a French-Canadian married to a Salvadorean, homeschooling offers the best chance to raise triliterate children who speak French, Spanish, and English. She admits that many parents around her are intimidated by the task. To Alvarez, however, homeschooling represents "simply a continuation of all the learning activities we all do with our children before they join kindergarten, which is to play, to expand their knowledge by asking questions, to listen to them, to read every day from a variety of resources, all the while making sure that they target all the school subjects in both languages." (4)

Parents who homeschool agree that being able to teach academic vocabulary in the heritage language is a strong incentive to take charge of their children's education. Since they usually get through the appropriate lessons faster than teachers in a regular classroom, they can take advantage of the extra time together as a family to read and talk in the heritage language. But most parents agree that the first steps to homeschooling are to do your research, talk to other parents who have been homeschooling their children for a few years, and get all your concerns looked after before jumping into this challenging—and rewarding—adventure.

Dual-Language Programs

If parents want to give their children a bilingual education in school, there are several options. In the U.S., dual-language programs (also known as two-way immersion programs) are rapidly becoming popular because of their inclusive message: "Bilingualism For All."

According to the Center for Applied Linguistics, these programs "strive to promote bilingualism and biliteracy, grade-level academic achievement, and positive cross-cultural attitudes and behaviors in all students." (5) A typical classroom includes both native English and minority-language students, and the academic content takes place in both languages equally. According to CAL, in early 2009 there were 346 dual-language programs in 28 states, compared with 284 programs in 2004. (6)You can find a directory at CAL's website, www.cal.org/twi. Obviously if you find one in your community that targets your native language, you'll probably feel like you've just won the lottery! These programs are very popular and they fill up quickly, but they are still very scarce.

In addition to dual-language programs, there are total-immersion programs, especially in the early grades. From Boise, Idaho, to York, Maine, there are preschool teachers ready to play, sing, and dance with your children solely in your native language! For example, the Bambini Immersion Preschool in Glendale, Arizona, offers all-day or half-day immersion programs in Spanish or Mandarin. The preschool—founded by a parent who believes in "preparing children to become global citizens in the 21st century!"—also has afterschool programs to reinforce the children's language skills. In Winnetka, Illinois, children can attend a French preschool for a half day of songs and stories that explore French culture. The three-year program was created by the French Ministry of Education in 2003. To research total-immersion programs by state, grade level (from kindergarten to grade 12), and language, go to www.cal.org/resources/immersion. The site also includes partial-immersion programs available across the country.

Developmental Bilingual Education Programs

The subject of bilingual education in the public schools is complex and deserves more space than I can give it here. If you want to understand its history and development, there have been many expertly-written books published in recent years. I recommend Ofelia García's book titled *Bilingual Education in the 21st Century: A Global Perspective,* as well as *The Care and Education of Young Bilinguals* by Colin Baker. You can also contact the National Association for Bilingual Education or any of its twenty three affiliates around the country.

According to Professor Stephen Krashen, a well-known advocate for bilingual education, "We need to distinguish two distinct goals of bilingual education. The first is the development of academic English and academic success, the second is the development of the heritage language." As he points out, "Most of the debate has been about the first goal." (7)

When we look at the second goal of bilingual education, much of the research shows that when children are offered developmental programs (also called "late-exit"), they have a better chance to maintain and progress in their first language, keep close family ties, learn English well, and grow up with a more integrated sense of self. Along with dual language programs, they successfully promote what we all wish for our children: bilingualism and biliteracy.

The reality, unfortunately, is that most schools that offer bilingual education only offer "early exit" transitional programs that focus on quickly moving students from a curriculum taught in the child's native language to mainstream English-only classes. The emphasis is not on maintaining and progressing in the heritage language but on acquiring English as quickly as possible. Obviously that's not a good option for parents who want to raise bilingual children.

Many bilingual programs—mostly located in the Southwestern States—have suffered in the last few years as a consequence of state and federal policies like California's "English for the Children" Proposition 227 and Arizona's Proposition 203. Then, the Bilingual Education Act was replaced. The law had passed in 1968 to protect English language learners and give them a more sensible solution than the previous "sink or swim" method that had caused so many students to struggle academically or, worse, drop out of school. But unfortunately, in 2002, the law was replaced with Title III of the controversial No Child Left Behind Act and renamed "The English Language Acquisition, Language Enhancement, and Academic Achievement Act." Although the U.S. government has been outspoken in recent years about the critical need for fluent speakers of foreign languages, strangely enough these recent federal policies have taken away all mention of the importance of bilingualism and biliteracy and have stripped English language learners of the opportunity to maintain and progress in their heritage language. As Professor Wayne E. Wright, at the University of Texas in San Antonio, writes, "In this age of accountability, when all that matters is raising test scores, heritage language instruction is given a low priority." (8)

According to NABE, "Among the most serious [political attacks] to date are ballot initiatives in California, Arizona, and Massachusetts mandating English instruction for most children until they become fully proficient in English." The irony, as many scholars have noted, is that the demand for dual language programs, often serving middle class English-native speakers, has skyrocketed across the U.S., as more and more parents realize the critical need for bilingualism in the 21st century. The issues of power and race are evident in the context of bilingual education, but it's heartbreaking to know that, caught in the middle, are young students who think, feel, laugh, express themselves in one language and are told that, in order to add English to their knowledge, they must subtract their home language. Especially since this policy is a blatant contradiction to the scientific fact that learning a second language builds on proficiency in the first language. When students are encouraged to maintain and progress in their first language, they will learn English faster.

Fortunately there are countless educators, school administrators, parents, and community members who are all working tirelessly every day to see that all children get the opportunity to develop their world language skills. Since November 2008, many people have expressed their optimism about the new administration and its more inclusive views on bilingual education and heritage language maintenance. It is still too early, however, to see how President Obama's time in office will affect our bilingual children's school options.

In the meantime, it's important for parents to speak up about the language programs they would like to see implemented by their local school district. We can speak up for more dual-language programs and developmental bilingual education programs to encourage all children to grow up with the academic, social, cultural, and economic benefits of speaking more than one language. At the end of Chapter 10, I've included helpful tips—provided by Meagan Dawson M.ED., the principal of West View K-8, a dual language school in Burlington, WA—of specific steps parents can take to start a dual-language program in their own community.

HERITAGE LANGUAGE SCHOOLS

Some researchers believe that when it comes to language maintenance and identity formation, our best chances are still within our own family circles and the support networks we create. As Shuhan C. Wang and Nancy Green note in *Heritage Languages in America*, "The major responsibility lies with families and the heritage language groups themselves, who must mobilize the community to provide a network of home and community support for heritage language and cultural activities that take place outside of school." (9) In more and more communities, parents are keeping their children bilingual and in touch with their cultural traditions and beliefs by organizing heritage language programs after school.

Language schools require a high degree of commitment and dedication; parents are usually involved in all facets, from fundraising to teaching to acquiring materials. Books and materials are often purchased by the participating staff. Some programs are funded by foreign governments, but many others rely solely on private donations and small tuition fees. As in homeschooling, parents use a variety of resources for the curriculum, including CDs, DVDs, worksheets, posters, and flashcards. Through family contacts, consulates and embassies, parents sometimes can obtain traditional textbooks and other curricular materials. When possible, parents work in conjunction with university professors or international college students to strengthen the quality of instruction.

To see if there is a heritage-language program in your area, check the Alliance for the Advancement of Heritage Languages website. One of the organization's goals has been to compile an online list of heritage-language programs around the country. You can look up the list, which is divided by type and by language, at http://www.cal.org/heritage/profiles/view.html. Parents and educators can add a description of their own community's heritage-language program to the list, to expand the much-needed database. This is the organization's mission statement: "To promote societal multilingualism that will benefit individuals, communities, and the country as a whole, the United States needs effective policies, strategies, and resources that support heritage language development and maintenance as part of a comprehensive approach to language proficiency." (10)

New programs and centers are sprouting around the country, as more and more individuals and communities get involved in finding ways to preserve their linguistic and cultural heritage. For example, in September 2008, the Russian Maryland Cultural Center, Matryoshka, in Clarksville, opened its doors to the community. Members can learn the Russian language and discover the country's traditions, history, music, and folk dance. The center offers classes for children of all ages (as young as age 2) and adults in Russian language and literature, as well as lessons in folk dance, music, chess, arts and crafts, math, and history.

In Irvine, California, the Khayam Persian School Foundation offers after-school programs and extracurricular activities for students ages 6 through 12. Founded in 1982, the program aims to teach Iranian-American children the Persian language, including reading and writing, and Iranian cultural traditions. The students—mostly second-generation immigrants—attend classes once a week, with a special summer session that lasts six weeks and offers language lessons as well as Persian dance lessons.

Charter Schools

The headline of a 2008 *New York Times* front-page article read "Immigrants in Charter Schools Are Seeking the Best of Both Worlds." (11) For many parents who want to raise bicultural children, charter schools now offer a place to learn where the philosophy revolves around integration instead of assimilation. Children are encouraged to take pride in their heritage and cultural traditions, and the staff often has similar cultural and linguistic backgrounds to better bond with the children. According to the U.S. Charter Schools website, "Over one million students are enrolled in more than 3,500 schools in 40 states plus the District of Columbia and Puerto Rico" in 2009. (12) Charter schools are usually founded by parents and community organizers, teachers, entrepreneurs, or by existing public schools that choose to change their status. They are technically public schools, usually sponsored by the state or local school board, but they're independently run to give parents and teachers more flexibility and creative choices. International schools also are included under the umbrella of charter schools.

Although most public schools offer foreign-language classes, they often are only available in Spanish, French, or German. By contract, charter schools often offer classes in a wide variety of languages. The Charter schools in Florida, for example, offer classes in Mandarin, Hebrew, Italian, and Greek. Some charter schools offer more language immersion than others. For example, the new Pioneer Valley Chinese Immersion Charter School in Boston transitions students from seventy-five percent of classroom time in Mandarin in kindergarten and first grade to about fifty percent by eighth grade. All students also learn to write in Mandarin.

You can search detailed state profiles of existing schools on the U.S. Charter Schools website. It also offers a well-laid out step-by-step guide for communities that are interested in creating a new Charter school. For parents who are trying to keep their children bilingual and connected to their heritage, these schools can offer vital support.

Attending School in the Home Country

Many parents choose to supplement their native language input by giving their children first-hand cultural experience and enrolling them for an extended period in a school in their home country. Marjukka Grover, cofounder of the publishing company Multilingual Matters, has two adult bilingual sons and can attest to the success of this strategy. She shares her story: "When our boys were eight and ten, they stayed in Finland with my parents from Christmas through to Easter, attending the local primary school. That winter happened to be the coldest in Finland for a hundred years. It was hard to send them off to school on those cold, dark winter mornings, knowing that I soon had to leave them behind. However, the experiment worked well. Both Tommi and Sami learned to read and write in Finnish, and my parents got to know their grandsons better. Most of all the boys learned what it is like to be able ski, skate, play ice hockey—simply, what it is like to be a Finnish boy!" (13)

Whether children attend school in the home country for a month or a semester, the experience immerses them in the culture, reaffirms the importance of maintaining their heritage language, and gives them a chance to bond with children who share a similar background, as well as develop deeper and longer lasting ties to cousins and extended family. Overall, it gives them a better understanding of who they are.

As we explore the different school options to help our children learn to read and write in two languages, Professor Baker reminds us, "Bilingual children must be biliterate for their languages to have value, uses, and prospects . . . . Biliteracy aids chances of employment, achievement and enculturation." (13) It's important to keep this goal in mind because—as seasoned parents will attest—whatever decision we make, it will require courage, commitment, and perseverance. Whether we choose to homeschool part time or gather community support to open a new heritage school, Vern and I are excited to embark on this biliterate adventure as we watch our girls get ready for kindergarten!

CHAPTER 6

Bilingual *and* Recommended for English Honors

*It doesn't take a genius to see that nurturing the linguistic
and cultural resources of the nation is simply good
common sense in light of the cultural realities of the
21st century.*

Professor Jim Cummins, University of Toronto

At the end of ninth grade, two and a half years after I arrived in the U.S., I was recommended for tenth grade English honors. I was the only student in my class to receive this recommendation, and I remember feeling embarrassed since I was also the only non-English native among my classmates. But the feeling quickly turned to pride. I couldn't wait to get home to tell my parents. In retrospect, the fact that, as a student, I had spent so much time thinking about the English language, examining new words, and dissecting grammatical structures had made me a more attentive student. The recommendation lifted my self-esteem. I realized that I could speak French at home *and* do well in school. I didn't have to give up my native language.

There is still a prevalent thought in some sectors in the U.S. that, in order to excel in English, children need to give up their home language. This notion is easily overthrown by the success of millions of bilingual adults working in this country and around the world today. The attitude that English only matters is naïve and short-sighted in today's interconnected world. It has become evident that the sooner we accept bilingualism and multicultural awareness as an educational goal—for all children—the better equipped the next generation will be to work together, peacefully and productively.

The Cost of Losing a Heritage Language

When educators or administrators tell parents to give up speaking their native language to their children, they usually explain that doing so will enable the children to acquire English faster and adapt more easily to the new environment. It's a myth that is unfortunately widespread. There is no scientific evidence to show that losing the home language will help a child learn the language of the community. In fact, for most children, the loss of a native language can cause great emotional, social, cultural, and academic difficulties, with consequences that will be felt well into adulthood. They can include:

- **Low self-esteem and lack of self-confidence** As a newcomer, a child struggles to express her thoughts and feelings in the new language as she adjusts to a different environment. The rules have changed, and she has to learn them through trial and error, which means she can feel insecure and ignorant. She may even be ridiculed by peers. (I'm just speculating here!) It's a difficult stage, during which self-confidence can quickly spiral down. In addition, when their first language is not recognized or is devalued, children are forced to deny a part of who they are.

- **Severed family ties** For most children, losing a heritage language means losing contact with grandparents and meaningful relationships with cousins, aunts, and uncles. It means being denied their oral history and the wisdom of their elders. Some children become so detached from their relatives that they lose sight of their family's values and cultural traditions. The gap grows and isolates children because they can't relate to their native cultural group.

- **Identity crisis** Without a sense of belonging, or a way to identify themselves, children feel marginalized. Without the right guidance and consideration from parents, teachers, and the community around them, they become lost. Without a clear path, they sometimes lack ambition and productivity; when they get older they might abuse alcohol and drugs to escape their reality; they struggle in school or, worse, drop out; the desperation can even lead to depression or thoughts of suicide. As philosopher Charles Taylor reminds us, recognition for who you are "is not just a courtesy we owe to people. It is a vital human need." (1)

- **Behavioral problems** Children who suffer from a low sense of self-worth, who don't have a clear sense of who they are, and who feel discriminated against can develop delinquent and antisocial behaviors. Research shows that when a community, or society in general, has a negative reaction toward a child's heritage language and culture, that child often develops feelings of inferiority, confusion, resentment, and anger, which can sometimes lead to aggressive behaviors.

- **Difficulty making friends** Even a monolingual child can struggle to make friends in school; when a child is just learning

English, it can be depressingly difficult. I was grateful for the French friends I had in school, as well as my sisters, for keeping me company as I gradually established friendships in English. Younger children and toddlers usually have an easier time making friends, even with a language barrier, but in middle and high school, relationships are more complicated. It's important for children to have peers to whom they can relate, who speak the same native language, as they adjust to their new environment. One young student, Romina, from Uzbekistan, describes her transition to a U.S. school: "I would cry every day when I first came and always wanted to go back home. I had none of my friends here, and I didn't understand the language. People also treated me differently because I dressed and acted different and I didn't speak English. Most of my friends were Russian. It was good that there were a lot of family members and Russian people living in my city." (2)

- **Poor academic performance** Research shows that when children maintain and progress in their native language, they will acquire English more easily. Dr. Krashen explains, "One would think that the more English children hear and read, the faster they will acquire it. This is not so. When we give children a good education in their first language, they get two things: knowledge and literacy. Both the knowledge they develop in the first language and the literacy they develop in their first language help English language development enormously. The effect is indirect, but powerful." (3) In addition, the argument that maintaining a first language while learning English will cause a higher dropout rate is unfounded. Studies show that the dropout rate is highly influenced by other sociocultural factors, including how long a child has been in the U.S., her access to books, parental supervision after school, family disruptions, and teen pregnancy. (4)

- **Learning English from parents who don't speak the language very well** It's critical to have every child learn at least one language fluently. If parents continue to speak their native language, they have the opportunity to strengthen their child's native language skills. In order to develop language proficiency, children need to live in an enriched language environment at home. If parents give up using their native language with their children and switch to a weaker language, their interactions will be less sophisticated in vocabulary, concepts, and thinking.

- **Emotional upheaval** We choose the language in which we want to bond with our children; it shouldn't be imposed on us. When I was busy with one a.m., three a.m., and five a.m. feedings when my daughters were infants, I chose to nurture and care for them in French. It would be impossible for me today to suddenly switch to English full time simply because my children are starting school. If the language we use to express love goes away, children can feel confused and rejected.

It is short-sighted and hurtful to ask a parent to give up speaking her native language with her children when you consider all of these damaging consequences. Imagine for a moment what happens to an individual who gives in to the pressures and decides to assimilate and give up his heritage language. Unfortunately, he still hasn't mastered English completely, has not yet been included into the mainstream, and has not yet been given access to all the resources available to others in the community. It's a depressing but common scenario, and it's especially painful when it happens to children who are wrongly guided down this path. Children have nothing to hold on to, no "thread of continuity." As Professor Francesco Cavallaro, at Nanyang Technological University in Singapore, points out in his research, "This attitude is reflected in the negative self-image and low self-esteem of the minority group who has undergone this process, the sense felt within the group of being discriminated against, and feeling of disaffection and marginalization, along with not belonging to the mainstream culture and not having a culture or language of their own. It comes as no surprise that these features are coupled with relatively high rates of unemployment and delinquency." (5)

Instead, when children are given the support and the resources they need to maintain their native language and cultural heritage, they have the opportunity to build on their existing skills instead of subtracting acquired knowledge and losing an important part of who they are. Keeping a heritage language does not make English less important. The two can coexist peacefully. Most immigrants and global nomads understand that it is vital for children to excel in English. The ability to communicate effectively in the dominant language of the country opens many doors, socially, financially, and culturally. As President Barack Obama stated during his campaign, "Instead of worrying about whether immigrants can learn English—they'll learn English—you need to make sure your child can speak Spanish. You should be thinking about how can your child become bilingual. We should have every child speaking more than one language. We should want our children with more knowledge. We should want our children to have more skills. There's nothing wrong with that. It's a good thing." (6)

For parents raising bilingual children, it's comforting to have a president who has lived abroad (Indonesia), who has multiple cultural references, and who values languages. But we have to acknowledge that bilingualism in the United States is still a difficult subject. For many Americans it has negative connotations because of the ugly debates around the country on bilingual education and the fear of the unknown that kicks in when people see their neighborhoods changing. There are also misguided and hurtful political views that protest, "Why should I learn the language of millions of illegal aliens?"

Some people are simply missing the point. It is not unpatriotic to speak two or three languages. Just the opposite. It makes us better leaders in almost every field. It makes us better prepared to reach out to the rest of the world. Census statistics indicate that out of the fifty-four million people who speak a language other than English at home, twenty percent—or eleven million—are school-age children. (7) If we don't value their native languages and promote their development, we're also taking away their chances at a better job, a more inclusive perspective, better community relations, stronger family ties, a well-defined identity, and a strong sense of self-worth.

As author Pico Iyer eloquently writes, "Anyone who steps out of the U.S. today, in any direction, quickly sees that the American Century has become the Global Century and that where a generation ago much of the globe was trying to look like America, now it's America that needs to get in tune with the rest of the globe." (8) This shift is going to help parents like us, no doubt, in terms of societal support and resources. But we still hold the responsibility to speak our heritage languages daily with our children. We need to get creative to keep our languages alive. We need to regularly remind our children of the benefits of speaking two languages and having a multicultural perspective. We can also make a difference by creating a supportive relationship with teachers and school administrators in our community.

The Importance of Parent/Teacher Conferences

The question for many parents is: How do we work with our children's teachers to help them understand and promote our family's cultural background and language goals? We often hear stories about successful leaders—in any field—who remember a particular teacher who changed the course of their lives. In his bestselling memoir *Angela's Ashes*, author Frank McCourt, who attended school in Ireland, had this to say about his teacher: "Mr. O'Halloran can't lie. He's the headmaster . . . . He says, You have to study and learn so that you can make up your own mind about history and everything else but you can't make up an empty mind. Stock your mind, stock your mind. It is your house of treasure and no one in the world can interfere with it. . . . You might be poor, your shoes might be broken, but your mind is a palace."(9) Teachers provide guidance, become mentors, and help shape the minds of our young, impressionable children. Teachers often spend more time with our children than we do! It's therefore vital to work with them. Although it's ultimately our parental responsibility to help our children excel in two (or more) languages, it never hurts to have dedicated teachers and school administrators on our side. The bigger the support group, the better.

A teacher who has personal experience with learning a foreign language—whether or not it matches his students' heritage languages—will be more supportive of a student's potential bilingualism. In addition, a teacher who has had proper training and is sensitive to and curious about different cultural values and perspectives will better foster an inclusive and respectful classroom. However, as they learn more about the U.S. school culture, parents can also make valuable contributions with a few effective steps, especially during parent/teacher conferences. These meetings can help both parties understand one another better. Here are some helpful tips for getting the most out of the conferences:

- Share your reasons and motivations for speaking your native language at home and for raising a bilingual child. One parent told me she successfully approached her child's teacher with research findings on childhood bilingualism to help the teacher understand its cultural value and academic benefits.

- Be aware of your culture-based perspective and try to better understand the school culture in the U.S. There are excellent books such as *American Ways: A Guide for Foreigners Living in the U.S.*, by Gary Althen; *Living in the U.S.A.*, by Alison Lanier;

and others that can give newcomers a better sense of how the U.S. school system operates. When parents have a better understanding of how their cultural values differ from the values promoted in school, they can have a more honest dialogue with teachers to help their children's integration.

- Clarify your family's multicultural background and share what the school system was like before for your child to give teachers a better understanding of your child's past experiences.

- Ask questions. Although this approach is easier for some parents than others, depending on their cultural backgrounds and personalities, asking questions and being open to the teachers' responses will help set up a much-needed line of communication when parents are unsure of how to proceed. For example, when dealing with an American tradition such as the prom, it can be helpful to get some clarification on how to survive the event!

- If there are other heritage language speakers in your community, talk to the school staff about how to get the kids together after school to practice their language skills in a fun and relaxed environment.

- Volunteer to speak at your child's school about your country and its cultural traditions and practices. The knowledge and skills that parents can share in the classroom are valuable resources for teachers and can serve as a welcome addition to the curriculum. Depending on the grade, this sharing of information can go well beyond simply discussing food and festivals. (But baking a traditional German gingerbread house or distributing *mithai*, or Indian sweets, is often welcomed!) Professor Baker lists the wide range of unexpected contributions parents can make, based on their particular work and experience in their home country. He writes, "Funds of useful knowledge include agricultural information about flowers, plants and trees, seeds, water distribution and management, animal care and veterinary medicine, ranch economy, car and bicycle mechanics, carpentry, masonry, electrical wiring and appliances, fencing, folk remedies, herbal cures and midwifery, archaeology, biology and mathematics." (10)

• Reach out and invite your child's teacher to share a traditional meal at your home to give her a glimpse of how your family communicates (translate when necessary!) and what traditions your family holds dear. Many cultural misunderstandings stem from a simple lack of awareness and knowledge. When we reach out to our children's school staff, we will develop better relations and improve our children's academic success.

The Future of Our Native Languages

Even with all of our hard work at home and our well-thought-out schooling decisions, the statistics on sustaining a second language are grim. It has often been noted that heritage languages can disappear within three generations. In May 2006, Ruben G. Rumbaut, a sociologist at the University of California at Irvine, presented discouraging research findings to the U.S. House Judiciary subcommittee on immigration. Rumbaut and his team interviewed 1,900 children of immigrants as part of a larger study; they found that "while 87 percent grew up speaking another language at home, only 34 percent said they spoke it well by adulthood. And nearly 70 percent said they preferred to speak English." (11) A common pattern for many young immigrants is to grow up monolingual in their native language, become bilingual for a short while as they adjust to living in a new culture, and then go back to being monolingual, but this time in the dominant language. Even for children who are exposed to two languages from birth, the start of school in English, monolingual friends, and television, video games, and the Internet in the dominant language often slow the development of their heritage language, no matter how diligently parents speak it at home.

DEALING WITH DISCRIMINATION

In addition to the widespread use of English in all arenas, English-only policies contribute to the difficulty of retaining a heritage language in the U.S. At the heart of linguistic discrimination, we all know, is not a fear that English will become less relevant, but a fear of someone who sounds different, someone whose beliefs, behaviors, and assumptions might not match ours. As senior analyst with research firm Common Sense Advisory, Nataly Kelly points out, "Linguistic paranoia seems to have reached unprecedented levels in recent years, a phenomenon that would probably shock America's Founding Fathers. After all, they intentionally decided not to declare an official language for the United States, knowing full well that linguistic dominance in the world is often in flux, and that doing so could restrict the country's ability to both compete internationally and respond to domestic needs." (12)

Forever the optimist, I think that as more and more people are educated about the personal, educational, and societal benefits of sustaining our world languages, we will see a decline in language discrimination in the U.S. A promising sign is the First Family. When we look at the extended families of President Barack Obama and First Lady Michelle Obama, we have a more realistic picture of the language diversity in this country. Together, their families speak English, Indonesian, French, Cantonese, German, Hebrew, Swahili, Luo, and Igbo. (13) Another encouraging sign: Having a foreign-sounding name no longer evokes the same feelings of marginality that it used to; instead, it calls upon us to honor and respect our cultural heritage.

It's important for communities to work together to elevate the status of heritage languages. Negative attitudes toward foreign languages lead our children to use them less and less. French, I realize, is a well-respected language, even in monolingual communities, and its status is undoubtedly one of the reasons my parents were successful in raising three bilingual children. When strangers hear us speak French and comment on it, they usually praise my children's language skills, tell us how wonderful the language sounds, or express their regret that their own parents didn't teach them a second language when they were young. Unfortunately, many immigrants in this country, especially Latinos, have not received the same courtesy. Bilingual parent and California resident Rey M. Rodriguez remarks, "I want my children to be proud of who they are; and to help them, I need a community that signals that Spanish is important to their lives. It amazes me that a two-year-old boy can already grasp that English is the predominant language and that Spanish is secondary and less valued." (14) Sociolinguistic studies show that it is very difficult for children to acquire active command of a heritage language without the support of the community. As J. Michael Adams and Angelo Carfagna, authors of *Coming of Age in a Globalized World*, explain, "We need to confront our fears and adjust to new realities. And we must shape our institutions and the systems in which we operate to reflect these new realities." (15)

According to the Pew Hispanic Center, one in five students in public schools is now Latino. (16) The growing accessibility of educational material online, at local libraries, and in language schools make it possible for young children—Hispanic and non-Hispanic—to learn and progress in Spanish. It is now the fourth most common language in the world and is spoken by more than thirty-five million people here in the U.S. Children should be encouraged to learn Spanish since there will be great opportunities for them to use it as professional adults.

PROMISING CHANGES

Today awareness is growing, at the local, state, and federal levels, of the economic, political, educational, social, and cultural benefits of speaking a second language. The reality is that bilingualism is now a requirement in today's interconnected world. As Professor Jim Cummins bluntly states, "Students who grow up and are educated in a monocultural cocoon risk becoming social misfits, totally unprepared for the world of work or play in the 21st century." (17)

In 2004, the Department of Defense hosted its first National Language Conference to discuss strategies for helping citizens become more culturally aware and language proficient, so that the U.S. can retain its leadership role in a more globalized world. Its resulting "Call to Action" report recommended that federal, state, and local government agencies, academic institutions, and businesses "provide opportunities for individuals from our many ethnic heritage communities to maintain, enhance, and use their heritage languages to their own and the Nation's benefit." The Department of Defense report states, "There is an urgent need for a national strategy on foreign languages and cultural competency" and adds that "the potential that heritage speakers bring to our schools can present a national asset to be developed." (18) Governmental agencies, business leaders, policymakers, school administrators, and teachers are now focused on reversing the tide and making sure students are encouraged to maintain, and progress in, their first- and second-language skills. As Joy Kreeft Peyton, Donald A. Ranard, and Scott McGinnis, the editors of *Heritage Languages in America: Preserving a national resource*, write, "Traditionally, the United States has ignored its non-English languages. Today, at a time when the nation critically needs world citizens— men and women who can function in more than one language and one culture—our many ethnic languages constitute a rich linguistic and cultural resource that we can no longer afford to neglect." (19)

Teachers, business leaders, community organizers, and politicians are taking important steps to ensure the maintenance of world languages in the U.S. Here's a short list of encouraging developments:

- **Task Force for the Preservation of Heritage Language Skills, Maryland**

  The Maryland state legislature is the first in the country to set up a task force in charge of investigating how to develop better resources and opportunities for heritage language speakers. According to Joy Kreeft Peyton, the vice-president of the Center for Applied Linguistics, "The bottom line is [Maryland has] switched the focus from immigrants as a problem to people with high-level skills, high levels of education, and speaking languages other than English. It's a different focus that is very powerful." (20) The recommendations, to be implemented by the State Department of Education, include providing more children's books in heritage languages at public libraries and in schools; helping heritage speakers become teachers; adding more dual-language programs throughout the state; and providing foreign-language credit to high school students who speak another language than English at home. Hopefully more states will follow suit.

- **Study Abroad Foundation Act—S.473**

  This bill passed by the House of Representatives and now waiting for a Senate vote dramatically increases the number of American students who will study abroad. In 1996–1997, fewer than 100,000 students studied abroad for credit. In 2006–2007, the number jumped to 241,791. The bill plans to increase the number to one million students in the next ten years, by offering more program opportunities to more diverse students and to more diverse destinations. As the associate executive director of public policy for the National Association of Foreign Student Advisors (NAFSA), Victor C. Johnson, explains, "U.S.

citizens who have never been abroad except on guided tours to tourist attractions cannot be the foreign policy constituency that our leaders seek. Those who have spent some time studying and learning abroad, who have developed an interest in a foreign country or region, who have friends there, and who speak their language, can be and will be." (21)

The bill comes at a time when language-class enrollments in colleges and universities are up by thirteen percent, according to the Modern Language Association. The latest survey shows that between 2002 and 2006, enrollments in Arabic classes have increased by 127 percent. Enrollments in Chinese classes are up by fifty-one percent, and American Sign Language by thirty percent. (22)

- **National Language Coordination Act of 2009—S.1010**
  Introduced on May 7, 2009, by Senator Daniel Akaka (D-HI), this bill would establish a much-needed National Foreign Language Coordination Council in the Executive Office of the President. The Council would be directed by a National Language Advisor, appointed by the President, "to oversee, coordinate, and implement continuing national security and language education initiatives." (23) For more information on these bills, you can log on to the Joint National Committee on Languages & the National Council for Languages and International Studies website cited above. You can also log on to http://thomas.loc.gov to find out the status of a bill as it waits for a Congress vote. You are also encouraged to call or write to your local representatives to speak up about the importance of supporting our world languages.

- **Reauthorization of Title VI of the Higher Education Act**
  The programs included in this law promote the importance of foreign languages by:
  - extending support to students, in a variety of disciplines, who study foreign languages

- offering loan forgiveness to students who become language teachers
- establishing the position of Deputy Assistant Secretary of Foreign Language and International Education in the Office of Post-Secondary Education

- **The Heritage Language Initiative**
  In 1999, the National Foreign Language Center and the Center for Applied Linguistics created the Alliance for the Advancement of Heritage Languages. The organization has developed a fantastic website at www.cal.org/heritage with updates on initiatives, resources, and discussions happening around the country. One of its missions is to offer parents a comprehensive list of heritage language programs in community-based organizations, public schools, and universities to give families the tools they need to maintain their native language. It also invites the staff of language programs, who can submit their profile online, to learn from another by sharing advice, methods, and ideas.

- **The National Heritage Language Resource Center**
  Funded by the U.S. Department of Education, the center is dedicated to heritage language education. It works to develop materials and curriculum for teachers who have heritage language learners in their classrooms. It also publishes the online *Heritage Language Journal*. There are currently fifteen national Language Resource Centers across the U.S., located at major universities, each dedicated to improving the teaching and learning of foreign languages.

- **National Language Service Corps**
  If you speak Hausa, Hindi, Indonesian, Russian, Swahili, Mandarin, Vietnamese, Thai, or Marshallese, the staff at NLSC wants to meet you! As Dr. Robert Slater, Director of the National Security Education Program, explains, "The National Language

Service Corps is an organization of Americans who have a certifiable level of language ability who are willing and able to serve the Federal government when their skills are needed." (24) This new organization is the first of its kind and it will certainly open doors to better intercultural relations and communication in our communities. You can check out their website at www.nationallanguageservicecorps.org for more information.

- **Discover Languages . . . Discover the World!**
  The American Council on the Teaching of Foreign Languages (ACTFL) created this new initiative in 2006 to raise public awareness about the importance of foreign language education in this country. The program has a broad reach; it works with teachers, parents, community leaders, businesses, and policymakers to promote language skills. Such programs are vital because they promote the idea that our native languages open doors to more academic success and career opportunities. They also help us secure the societal support and resources we need to successfully raise bilingual children.

CHAPTER 7

The Benefits of Bilingualism (for extra motivation on days when the English-only movement doesn't sound so unreasonable!)

Americans who travel abroad for the first time are often shocked to discover that, despite all the progress that has been made in the last 30 years, many foreign people still speak in foreign languages.

Author and former Miami Herald humor columnist Dave Barry

Although we all have our unique stories about how we became bilingual families, I would venture that, for most of us, raising our children to speak two languages is a necessity. It keeps us connected as a family. We nurture our children in the language that feels the most natural. We share our values, beliefs, and view of the world.

We pass on our life lessons to the next generation. When my sister's children living in Cambodia call on Skype and exchange evening greetings in French in front of the webcam, there's a feeling of relief and gratitude that our daughters can communicate with them. (Even if they're just showing off their latest Play-Doh sculptures!)

It's impossible for me to imagine that someone outside the family unit—a politician, a pediatrician, a neighbor—would ever advise me to give up speaking French to my children. Unfortunately, thousands of parents regularly encounter resistance from individuals, usually monolinguals, who insist that children should focus on English only and, consequently, give up all the rewards of becoming bilingual.

Children need a positive learning environment in which their heritage language is valued and they are praised and encouraged as they learn. Luckily, as parents, we still have a strong determining influence. Researchers agree that our attitudes and beliefs as parents are key factors in sustaining our world languages. This chapter aims to remind us of the lifelong benefits of bilingualism and the unique potential of every bilingual child. I hope it also helps us dismiss the naysayers in our lives, who might not understand what they're asking us to forfeit if we stop using our native language with our children.

Bonding as a Family

When I moved to New Jersey from Compiegne, France, at age twelve, I spoke only a handful of English words. I remember standing in the principal's office trying to put a complete sentence together, but all I could muster was "I France!" That's how limited my English was. I would love to say that I had a certain penchant for learning, but the reality is that I had dedicated parents who found a way to help their daughters maintain their French *and* excel in English.

Every day after school, my parents, my sisters and I spent time at the kitchen table discussing our homework—first in French, and then slowly in both languages. (A good dose of culture shock made us want to stay close to home, even if it meant studying!) At a time when some parents struggle to find common ground with their young teenagers, families who learn a second language together often have an opportunity to strengthen their relationship. (My husband and I have a pact: when the girls become teenagers, we're moving to Vietnam!)

So unbeknownst to my sisters and me, during our first couple of years in the U.S., we were already reaping some of the benefits of learning a second language. We bonded as a family. My sisters and I would meet up in the school cafeteria to puzzle over the pronunciation of new words such as *hypothesis, thorough* (the "th" is very tricky for French native speakers!), and the troublesome *hierarchy*. We compared notes and cringed at the constant mispronunciation of our last name and the not-so-gentle nicknames we were given by classmates. Back home, we enjoyed teasing our parents about their sharp French accent when they spoke English.

Academic Skills

In the last few years, experts have shown that speaking two languages can greatly enhance students' academic success. The unique brain-power involved in switching languages, according to circumstances or audience seems to trigger a mental agility that has amazing consequences. For example, researchers have found a strong correlation between speaking two languages and the ability to focus. According to Professor Bialystok, the fact that bilinguals must constantly choose which language to use and which language to put aside puts in place a mechanism in the brain that may also help us make decisions quickly, multitask efficiently, and even keep our memory sharp. (1)

With brain-imaging tools, such as MRIs, scientists have been able to look at the brain activity of bilingual adults who use both languages daily. They have found that the area controlling our attention and focus is more prominently activated. This activity, according to the Society for Neuroscience, is so prominent and predictable on brain scans that it serves as a "neurological signature" for bilingualism! (2) Scientists have found that bilinguals who've been exposed to a second language since age five have more dense grey matter in the brain sections in which language skills operate. This new finding, according to scientists, confirms that the structure of the brain is significantly altered by exposure to two languages from an early age.

As Dr. Suzanne Flynn, professor of linguistics at the Massachusetts Institute of Technology, explains, "[Bilingual children] are better able to block out extraneous 'noise' and successfully deal with incoming information without getting distracted or derailed."(3) When your daughter is conducting research on the Internet for a history project, it's good to know that her bilingualism is working for her!

The correlation between bilingualism and the ability to concentrate has also motivated a group of researchers to investigate if learning a second language could potentially help children with Attention Deficit Hyperactivity Disorder, and extensive studies are currently under way. (Look for updates on this book's website, www.bilingual bychoice.com.)

The benefits of bilingualism also cross over to sometimes unexpected academic subjects such as science and math. Bilingualism helps children develop stronger analytical and problem-solving skills, such as the mental agility to drop one concept and try another one out. (4)

Higher SAT Scores

When it comes to the two most important high school exams, several studies have proved that students who study a foreign language for at least four years score significantly higher on the reading, math, and writing sections of the Scholastic Achievement Test (SAT) and the American College Test (ACT) than students with no foreign language instruction. (5) Considering the pressure and high stakes surrounding these tests, this finding is persuasive news for both bilingual families *and* parents who are thinking about enrolling their monolingual children in a foreign-language class.

Access to More Knowledge

For the bilingual reader, there is also the incredible opportunity to tap into the rich history and literature of two countries. As children grow, they learn to compare and contrast how people act and react, how they relate to one another and to the world around them, and what they eat, wear, and talk about around the dinner table. At our house, the literature today mostly revolves around *Petit Ours Brun* (Little Brown Bear) and Juliette, but as Natasha and Sofiya grow, I look forward to sharing my favorite French authors with them.

Many bilingual adults I spoke with described their enthusiasm for reading international newspapers online. The media have a powerful influence on how people think about and react to political news; bilingual readers are equipped to track down different angles to a story and draw their own conclusions. Being bilingual helps children and young adults to deepen their understanding of the world around them. Students can use their language skills to better understand current events and make sharper analyses.

Self-Esteem

Research shows that children will grow up with a better sense of self when they are aware of their heritage and active in the traditions of their cultures. When we share our heritage culture and language with our children, we give them the chance to understand who they are as a whole. Through our words and actions, we also teach them to respect and appreciate people from different cultural and linguistic groups. The activities in Chapters 9 and 10 will not only encourage your children's language skills, but they will also help children develop a positive relationship with their two cultures.

A Balanced Cultural Identity

By helping our children sustain their first language, we're securing their ties to their first cultural group, which will always remain an important part of who they are. They can keep in touch with friends back home, and with grandparents, cousins, aunts, and uncles; they can also keep up with the latest books, music, and movies. A healthy sense of self—knowing who you are and understanding where you came from—leads to a more integrated cultural identity. The key is to elevate the status of the language so that a child hears and sees that his close family and friends respect and value his languages. Being bilingual should give him a sense of pride and accomplishment.

Today, leaders in almost every field are calling for ways to educate U.S. children with more cultural awareness and sensitivity, and with fluency in more than one language, to keep up with the demands of a globalized world. Heritage-language speakers are leading the way! Encourage your child to sustain his first language and learn his new community language, and you will give him a better chance at a rewarding career.

Global-mindedness

Today it's imperative for young people to learn about different cultures and the wider world around them. As J. Michael Adams and Angelo Carfagna emphasize in *Coming of Age in a Globalized World*, "The need to understand globalization and to be able to respond and adapt is perhaps the most crucial challenge facing humanity . . . . The future depends on the next generation being able to collaborate across cultures and nations to forge global solutions." (6) Speaking a second language is a powerful tool to forge much-needed alliances. Whether it's an international group of scientists working together to develop a flu vaccine, or engineers helping to rebuild part of a city, or researchers attacking global warming, we need to understand one another to be effective partners.

College Preparation

To produce well-educated, globally minded students, more and more universities and colleges require proficiency in a foreign language for admission. When our children fill out their college applications, their bilingualism (or, by then, perhaps trilingualism) will be an asset. The academic and business worlds are now looking for graduates who can communicate effectively in more than one language and who can understand the nuances and cultural contexts of a language. It's evident that heritage-language speakers will have more linguistic prowess than someone who learns a second language later on in school. (Which doesn't mean that children should not be encouraged to learn a second language at any age. But earlier is better!) In addition, research shows that it is easier for bilinguals to learn a third language than for monolinguals to learn a second language. (7)

Some bilingual students also report that they have an easier time making the transition to college. When children relocate internationally during their childhoods, they often develop practical skills to cope with a new situation and integrate into a new setting. These skills, when properly fostered, can translate into smoother transitions, including the transition between high school and college. Additionally, students often use these cross-cultural skills as they reach out to newcomers on campus, even if they don't speak the same language. They learn to work with different cultural groups, listen attentively to different perspectives, and serve as a bridge to people who struggle to communicate with one another. These skills will make our children better leaders in any field they choose to pursue.

Competitive Advantage in the Workplace

Speaking two languages will also greatly influence a student's job search. Numerous surveys of business and industry leaders and human-resource managers confirm that speaking a foreign language gives graduates a competitive advantage in the workplace. According to the Committee for Economic Development (CED), a survey of large U.S. corporations revealed that "Almost 80 percent of the business leaders . . . expected their overall business to increase notably if they had more internationally competent employees on staff." (8) Bilinguals can also qualify for exciting short- or long-term job assignments in other countries, some of which are not accessible to monolinguals.

As the CED explains, "Employees who demonstrate cultural competence"—which requires "a combination of foreign language skills, international knowledge, and international experience"—"are more likely to be selected for and perform well on global teams, which can lead to greater success and advancement within the organization."

For my sister Brigitte, her bilingualism and cultural competence served her well when she was hired as an aeronautical engineer at the world's largest satellite launch company, Arianespace. Although its headquarters are in Evry, France, its launch site is in French Guyana in South America, where my sister lived for ten years. The Ariane rocket—used to launch the commercial satellites—arrives in French Guyana in multiple stages, each from a different European country. The stages are then put together and tested by the crew on site. This kind of work demands a high level of cross-cultural skills and proficiency in foreign languages. As Engineer in Mechanical Propulsion, Brigitte greatly contributed to Arianespace's global team—including its European partners and clients from around the world—because of her ability to work and communicate effectively with people from different cultures.

With the world's economies becoming more and more entangled, with technologies and communications connecting every corner of the world, English-only seems less and less adequate—or profitable. Growing up in Westfield, New Jersey, in the 1980s, I often heard that it made sense for Europeans to learn foreign languages because we all lived so close to one another, but that for Americans, English was the only language necessary, since the United States was physically isolated. Considering the global migration of the last three decades, this argument is no longer sustainable. (It didn't seem sensible back then, either!) There are now more than fifty-four million people in the U.S. who speak a language other than English at home, according to the 2007 American Community Survey. The U.S. Census bureau predicts a 213 percent increase in the Asian population by 2050, which translates to 33.4 million people. It also predicts that by 2050 Hispanics will make up twenty-five percent of the population. As a consequence, the U.S. will continue to see a high demand for Spanish-speaking educators and bilingual teachers. (9) In December 2008, the media reported that the Pentagon is struggling to find linguists and culture experts to help carry out various missions around the world. Arabic speakers, as well as Turkish, Somali, Korean, and others, are always in high demand in government posts.

When the U.S. Department of Defense organized its National Language Conference in 2004, its "Call to Action" report stated, "[If] the United States is to remain a global power in business, education and international affairs, we need to immediately and drastically change how we value and teach foreign languages." (10) Today, leaders in almost every field realize that it's been unproductive and detrimental to try to dismiss the more than 300 languages spoken in the U.S. (11) This awareness and sense of urgency from organizations, schools, corporations, and government agencies helps us greatly as parents, as we widen our support network to raise our children to value their languages and their cultural backgrounds and finally reap all the benefits of being bilingual and multicultural.

Here's a list of careers in which languages are an asset.

Careers in Languages

Compiled by The Career Development and Gloria S. Williams Advisement Center, William Paterson University in New Jersey

Analyst	Export/Import Representative
Archivist	Filmmaker
Art Dealer	Foreign Correspondent
Assistant Production Manager	Foreign Diplomat
Bilingual Officer/Teller	Foreign Credit Manager
Bilingual Educator	Foreign Exchange Trader
Book Dealer	Foreign Service Officer
Bookkeeper	Foreign Service Peacekeeper
Buyer	Foreign Social Worker
Cataloger	Fund Raiser Coordinator
CIA Agent	Homeland Security Officer
Clergy	Human Resources Director
Civil Service Employer	Immigration/Naturalization Officer
College Professor	Insurance Sales Representative
Commercial Attaché	Intelligence Researcher
Consultant	Intelligence Specialist
Consumer Liaison	International Conference Planner
Public Relations Liaison	International Consultant
Copywriter	International Education Director
Cultural Attaché	International Flight Attendant
Cultural Officer	Journalist
Customs/Immigration Officer	Lawyer
Defense Intelligence Agent	Library Technician
Drug Enforcement Agent	Linguist
Editor	Media Specialist
Embassy Personnel	Missionary
Escort/Guide	Multilingual Receptionist

Museum Curator	Red Cross Employee
National Security Officer	Reporter
Negotiator	Researcher
Overseas English Language Media	Salesperson
Overseas Plant Manager	Scientific Linguist
Paralegal	Scientific Translator
Peace Corps Volunteer	Supervisor
Philanthropic Administrator	Teacher
Police Officer	Technical Writer
Politician	Telecommunications
Production Supervisor	TESO/ESL Teacher
Proofreader	Travel Agent/Tour Organizer
Publishing Specialist	Translator
Radio/TV Announcer	Travel Writer
Real Estate Agent	Writer

Intercultural Awareness

When we decide to raise our children to speak two or more languages, we give them access to a higher degree of cultural sensitivity and intercultural awareness, which grows from the early exposure to two sets of beliefs, behaviors, and assumptions. Many bilingual and multicultural students grow up with a wider view of the world. They grow up to be open to new experiences and lifestyles. They develop a cultural awareness that leads to more flexibility when they are confronted with different opinions and behaviors. In today's interconnected world, openness and flexibility are mandatory. Cultural awareness will help our children as they grow, in their personal friendships, in their community work, in their business ventures, in their travels, and anytime they encounter someone who sees the world in a different way. By raising our children to speak more than one language, we help them develop empathy and mindfulness. To quote Dr. Stella Ting-Toomey, author of *Communicating Across Cultures,* "Mindfulness means being . . .

aware of our own assumptions, viewpoints, and ethnocentric tendencies in entering any unfamiliar situation. Simultaneously, mindfulness means paying attention to the perspectives and interpretive lenses of dissimilar others." (13) We can help our children to become aware of their cultural identity and ready to listen to those who view themselves and the world differently.

We often hear the word *tolerance* in the media when people are discussing different cultural groups. I don't want to be "tolerated." I want to be accepted. If we do our job correctly, and succeed in keeping our children bilingual and open to different cultural ideas and opinions, we can hope to see our children one day develop not just tolerance, but a sincere appreciation for diversity.

CHAPTER 8

Listen Up!

Helpful Insights from Experts in Childhood Bilingualism and Second Language Acquisition and Encouraging Advice from Fellow Parents

It's easy to lose focus of the long-term benefits of growing up with two languages and two cultures when you're having a bad day—maybe your children are giving you grief for making them feel different or your in-laws are complaining about how your native language is hurting their English! This chapter will hopefully give you strength during these difficult moments. Throughout my research I have come across great quotes—a line or two that hit the mark—that remind me just how important it is that I stick with this goal for my children. They also remind me that, now, keeping my children bilingual becomes a group effort. We need the inspiration of seasoned parents who've successfully raised their children in two languages. We also need the brilliance of bilingualism advocates and researchers. Together, they remind us that our daily efforts at home are noticed; that we are not alone in this worthy endeavor; and that together we are giving the next generation the cultural and linguistics knowledge they will need to be creative, respectful and engaged citizens of the world.

If you would like to research the titles or websites mentioned below, please check the list of references at the end of the book for more extensive information.

LANGUAGE LOSS

"The most important relationship between language and culture that gets to the heart of what is lost when you lose a language is that most of the culture is in the language and is expressed in the language. Take it away from the culture, and you take away its greetings, its curses, its praises, its laws, its literature, its songs, its riddles, its proverbs, its cures, its wisdoms, its prayers. The culture could not be expressed and handed on in any other way. What would be left? When you are talking about the language, most of what you are talking about is the culture. That is, you are losing all those things that essentially are the way of life, the way of thought, the way of valuing, and the human reality that you are talking about."

Joshua A. Fishman, "What do you lose when you lose your language?" in G. Cantoni (Ed.), *Stabilizing Indigeneous Languages*

EVERYDAY COMMUNICATION

"There is no set of rules of how to talk to a child that can even approach what you unconsciously know. If you concentrate on communication, everything else will follow."

Catherine Snow and Charles A. Ferguson, *Talking to Children: Language Input and Acquisition*

"Family talk in the primary language is an important way to maintain and develop L1 (first language) for children. The talk refers to more

than just daily conversations. It can be thematic, covering a specific topic at a time (e.g., John Glenn's return to space after more than 30 years); it can be exploratory, digging deep into each other's minds (e.g., personal immediate/long-term goals, worries/desires); it can be an educational game, playing while talking (e.g., magic squares, math puzzles, et cetera). This kind of talk in L1 enlarges children's vocabulary, improves their ability to express themselves logically, and helps them appreciate the flavor of the language."

Xiaoxia Li, Assistant Professor of Chemistry, University of Hawaii, "How Can Language Minority Parents Help Their Children Become Bilingual in Familial Context? A Case Study of a Language Minority Mother and her Daughter," *Bilingual Research Journal*, Spring/Summer 1999

"Correct Spanish is the same Spanish your community speaks and understands. Children will learn forms that are appropriate in other environments when they are exposed to them. Encouraging your child to use Spanish whenever possible is one of the greatest contributions you can make to his/her personal and educational development."

Gordon J. Douglas, "Hablemos Espanol en Casa" (We Speak Spanish At Home), The New Mexico Association for Bilingual Education website

"I think the bottom line is that one only learns a language through immersion and everyday contact—specifically, situations wherein one is forced to use and learn the language to communicate. When there are easier options, those are generally taken."

"Be realistic and aware that it doesn't just happen by osmosis. It takes daily effort and sometimes hard choices. Putting my eighteen-month-old daughter into an entirely French daycare situation where, at least initially, no one would understand her and she would understand no one, took some commitment and faith on our part. She was quite unhappy for awhile but now functions well in French and likes 'school' very much."

Tim (American) and Lena (Swedish), raising children in France

As part of my research for this book, I set up a questionnaire online that parents could fill out anonymously to share their thoughts and advice on raising bilingual children. Here's a list of worthy daily reminders—good for taping on your fridge or your bathroom mirror!

"Be stubborn . . . they will thank you for it one day."

"Permit TV, but ONLY in the second language."

"Speak your own language and be true to yourself."

"Do not let the children dissuade you from speaking your own language to them, and don't put a time frame on anything—they'll absorb both languages in their own time and way."

"Don't worry about confusing them. Kids are incredibly smart. They might mix the languages at first, but they'll figure it out."

"Hang in there. Follow your heart, and keep going no matter what people say."

"Have a parent dedicated to a specific language. Worked for us . . . [our kids] easily switch from one language to another in the same conversation when addressing us both."

"Let it be natural. Don't force it on the children. Just let your enthusiasm for your language and culture be the driving force."

"Help your children make new friends by opening your home to fun sleepovers and get-togethers."

ENTHUSIASM

"There were some moments when we doubted whether it was worthwhile to start a new life in a foreign country or whether it was necessary to keep up the Chinese language in an English-speaking country. The doubt and hesitation watered down our enthusiasm in home bilingual activities. However, Amy always got excited and

studied effectively when I perked up and assured her of the advantage of being bilingual."

Xiaoxia Li, Associate Professor of Chemistry, University of Hawaii, "How Can Language Minority Parents Help Their Children Become Bilingual in Familial Context? A Case Study of a Language Minority Mother and her Daughter," *Bilingual Research Journal*, Spring/Summer 1999

READING AND LEARNING

"The child learns only what he is interested in, and the successful teacher is the one who can read, and respond imaginatively to, the interests of the child. The home also provides the most flexible schedule for learning. The caretaker can arrange activities to take advantage of the child's interests, can suspend activities just before a child loses interest, and can vary the program constantly to fit both the caretaker's and the child's needs. One of the best learning times has proved to be bedtime, when mother or father can read to the child, tell a story, sing a song, or play a game."

"The best teachers of reading are parents who are themselves most interested in reading."

"Tell your child stories, sing him songs, or play word games in the non-English language, especially at bedtime, stopping before he loses interest."

"Take your child to the public library at least once a week, get him a library card, check out some books, especially in his non-English language. Let him select his own books as much as possible."

Theodore Andersson, *A Guide To Family Reading in Two Languages: The Preschool Years*

"The more of the minority language the better; get as many books as you can!"

Anonymous

"Read at least one book on bilingualism. This way parents will feel more confident and ready for any challenge they might get from family/school/surroundings."

> Santi Dharmaputra, adult TCK raising two multilingual children

"Speak it all the time. Make the children answer back in their native language. Read in the native language."

> Isabelle Estrada, trilingual (Spanish/Italian/English) mother of two
> bilingual (Spanish/English) children

"I had access to a lot of books at home and read avidly anything I could get my hands on."

> Bianca Moebius-Clune, bilingual (German/English) adult

"Self-selected voluntary reading is beneficial and pleasant, and is highly effective. . . . For a fraction of what we are investing in testing, and in programs that clearly do not work, we could easily ensure that all children have access to quality reading."

> Stephen Krashen, "Ending All Literacy Crises,"
> *Language* magazine, May 2008

VISITS TO THE HOME COUNTRY

"We moved to the United States when the boys were six and five years old. At that time, they spoke English and German fluently. Each summer, we visited family in Germany and these visits were very useful for them to maintain their basic German skills. Their cousin is the same age so they spent a lot of time playing with his friends and had to make an effort to communicate. Watching movies and television and reading comics were also very helpful."

> Francoise Meissner, trilingual (German/French/English) mother of
> two multicultural teenagers

"Make sure to visit the country where the language comes from as often as you can, watch TV in that language, listen to music in that language, show pride in your culture."

Arlene Agosto, bilingual (Spanish/English) adult

SUPPORT SYSTEMS

"Vivian and I realized that if we wanted our children to be bilingual and bicultural, we couldn't do it alone. We needed a community of people. So we started looking around for Spanish language pro-grams . . . . Finally, a friend of mine discovered a small group of parents who met on a weekly basis at a local library . . . . The teachers were native-born speakers, and they were fantastic. They used beautiful books and melodic children's songs in Spanish to sing and dance to. Diego and Pablo, my second, learned about spring and named the days of the week and months of the year at their first class. Before I knew it, Diego was raising his hand because he understood the questions and wanted to participate . . . . And I was thrilled. The community that I was looking for existed, and by serendipity I had found it.

Rey M. Rodriguez, "Won't Your Spanish Hurt Their English," *LA Language World*, July 2007

"The best and easiest advice is to choose the right environment that is conducive to teaching your children more than one language (location, location, location). If this is not possible, then search for supportive groups that both the children and the parents can benefit from within their environment."

Anonymous

"Being German in the U.S. gives me an automatic connection to most other Germans in the U.S., and the same goes, somewhat, for Americans in other countries. Interestingly, it also gives me an automatic connection to any other person having moved to the

U.S. from another country, because I have an understanding of what it is like to not know the language and culture yet, and a deep understanding of the concept of culture as something that differs and can be shared, that's full of rich and interesting habits and perspectives that add to life and the many ways one can look at it."

Bianca Moebius-Clune, bilingual (German/English) adult

ADAPTING TO A NEW CULTURE

"My parents wanted desperately to keep us to the old standards, and yet they also wanted to see us succeed in this new culture. How could we study hard and earn all A's and get ahead but be sweet and submissive and let Papi make all the decisions? How could we remember our Spanish when we were forced to speak only English outside the home? How could we keep our mouths shut out of respeto for our parents when in school we were being taught to speak up and debate, if need be, with our teachers?"

Julia Alvarez, "Writers on America," U.S. Department of State: International Information Programs website

"The most compelling reason to learn the language of another land is because of the symbolic significance of the act of communication. At its most fundamental, the attempt to speak with people in a foreign country is an acknowledgement of their humanity and individual worth (as it is, perforce, an indication of our own), a sign that we take them and their concerns seriously."

Craig Storti, *The Art of Crossing Cultures*

"We often paper over our children's relocation challenges with reminders of how lucky they are to be moving abroad. That may be, but their childhood or adolescent concerns—like acceptance at a new school or by new friends, or having to leave a pet behind—are just as important to them as your job or your new house is to you. Be

available to them as much as possible during this transition period. If tears flow once in a while, that's all right, too. Children need to be allowed to feel their emotions without a parent's constant intellectualizing."

"The potential shock of new cultural customs can be turned into tremendous pleasure by approaching these as a wonderful by-product of life in the new country. This is an adventure, so get out there and explore."

"It's important to recreate, as quickly as possible, something familiar for your young children in your new home."

Robin Pascoe, *Raising Global Nomads: Parenting Abroad in an On-Demand World*

"For strong, loving lifetime attachments with your children, you have to work WITH the dominant culture in how you identify yourself."

"It is normal to have times when you may feel angry or depressed about the strength of the dominant culture's influence on your child even if you speak your native language exclusively at home. Take heart, talk to your spouse about the support each of you needs to have a balanced, honest approach to opening your heart to your own emerging biculturalism in the way you have opened to bilingualism . . . . You are on the cutting edge of the wave of multicultural families in this world of global mobility and multicultural appreciation."

Harriet Cannon, "Your Cultural Identity Changes As Your Child Grows," *Multilingual Living* magazine, March/April 2007

"Stress and anxiety (to say nothing of a permanent sinking heart) are conditions the normal, healthy person tries to avoid, whether at home or abroad. It's only natural, therefore, that if we find our encounters with the local culture stressful and otherwise unpleasant, we will begin to pull back from it. And by withdrawing and isolating ourselves from the culture, we seriously undermine any possibility of meaningful

adjustement; we can hardly adjust to that which we decline to experience."

Craig Storti, The Art of Crossing Cultures

IDENTITY

"My boys were born in Hong Kong and lived in Singapore before arriving to the U.S. Their father is Danish and I'm Egyptian/American. When they arrived to the U.S. at the age of 8 and 6, everyone at school kept asking them where they were from? (They had a pretty thick British accent and were very scandinavian looking.) After trying to explain themselves several times, they eventually just replied "We're Chinese!"

Myra Rasmussen, trilingual (English/Arabic/French) mother to
two multicultural teenagers

"I realized that I could make [language] perform. I had to believe the work was important to my being: To use my art as a bridge between my cultures. Unlike my parents, I was not always straddling. I began crossing the bridge, traveling back and forth without fear and confusion."

Judith Ortiz Cofer, poet and author, born in Puerto Rico and raised
in the U.S., Answers.com website

"People do not have roots, like plants. A person is mobile, free as the wind, and meant to manifest who they are wherever they happen to be."

LaDonna Harris, founder and former president of Americans
for Indian Opportunity, Foreword, Between Cultures: Developing
Self-Identity in a World of Diversity by H. Ned Seelye
and Jacqueline Howell Wasilewski

"While bilingualism and biculturalism may superficially appear to have a detrimental effect on identity, language does not cause identity problems. Rather, it is often the social, economic, and political

environment surrounding bilinguals that generates problems. It is not
bilingualism, but the condition in which that language community
lives that may be the cause of the problem. Where language
communities are oppressed and downtrodden, it is prejudice and
discrimination, not bilingualism, that affect identity."

Colin Baker, *The Care and Education of Young Bilinguals*

"A multicultural society is composed of people of many different
racial, ethnic, and cultural heritages. At its best, such a society and the
individuals within it recognize, accept, and value the diversity that
results from these cultures. The challenge for each of us as individuals
and as members of society is to find ways to integrate the diverse
threads of our identities into a consistent and workable whole without
diminishing the identity of those different from ourselves."

Elizabeth Pathy Salett, Diane R. Koslow, and Elsie Achugbue, *Race,
Ethnicity and Self: Identity in Multicultural Perspective*

"Children need a way to identify themselves. Parents of multicultural
kids need to give them self-descriptive words to use, rather than let
them wait for society to provide a label."

"Give children words and thoughts to combat racism or narrow-
mindedness of others."

Katy Abel, "Inventing Identities: Raising Multicultural Kids,"
Family Education website

"We all contain within ourselves multiple intersecting identities—
nationality, gender, sexual orientation, ethnicity and race, physicality,
native tongue, profession. In any given moment, one of those identities
may be more relevant to us than others. At the same time, the identities
in our backgrounds continue to make up the whole of who we are."

Barbara F. Schaetti and Sheila J. Ramsey, "The Global Nomad
Experience: Living in Liminality," Transition Dynamics website

"At one time I might have said, 'I have two hearts—one the U.S., and the other Cuba.' That was before I understood my own nature and being. Now I know that I have one heart, and that both countries are a part of it—one I chose, and the other chose me. Each has contributed to my being, my essence, and I rejoice and savor what both worlds have given and continue to give me . . . . I would not trade places with anyone—my life is too delicious!"

Teresa Bevin, bilingual author, Teresa Bevin website

RESPECTING DIFFERENT CULTURAL VALUES

"Parents who clash over child-rearing issues are often really battling over some basic difference in philosophy, values, or beliefs that they as a couple have not managed to resolve; the child merely provides the spark for the conflict. But these underlying issues are often difficult to recognize or define, let alone come to grips with; so, instead of going to the heart of the matter, the couple fights over the particulars."

Dugan Romano, *Intercultural Marriage: Promises and Pitfalls*

"It is not always easy to have your voice heard, because we all speak and hear through our own cultural values. Raised by my Comanche grandparents in rural Oklahoma, words and tones of voices were important and the only form of discipline we experienced. In raising my own children, I found that their Scots-Irish American father and his family used words and tones of voice very different from my Comanche relatives. I had to learn how to interpret his tones in a non-Comanche manner. Our children learned both types of communication."

LaDonna Harris, founder and former president of Americans for Indian Opportunity, Foreword, *Between Cultures: Developing Self-Identity in a World of Diversity* by H. Ned Seelye and Jacqueline Howell Wasilewski

"Our boys do definitely have a mix of cultural values, although the culture of the U.S. is certainly dominant. It's hard to pinpoint

examples because they have aborbed this mix as they have grown up. They accept the fact that things are done differently in different countries. They feel totally at home in three countries and three cultures—the U.S., Germany, and the U.K."

Francoise Meissner, trilingual (German/French/English) mother of
two multicultural teenagers

CITIZENS OF THE WORLD

"The future is here. It's multiethnic, multicultural, and multilingual. But are students ready for it?"

"The new skill set that students will need goes well beyond the United States' current focus on the basics and on math, science, and technology. These skills are necessary, of course, but to be successful global citizens, workers, and leaders, students will need to be knowledgeable about the world, be able to communicate in languages other than English, and be informed and active citizens."

Vivien Stewart, "Becoming Citizens of the World,"
Educational Leadership, April 2007

"The world is indifferent to tradition and past reputations, unforgiving of frailty and ignorant of custom or practice. Success will go to those individuals and countries which are swift to adapt, slow to complain, and open to change."

Andreas Schleicher, "The Economics of Knowledge: Why Education
is Key for Europe's Success, *Lisbon Council Policy Brief*, 2006

"If you look ahead five to ten years, the people with the top jobs in large corporations, even in the United States, will be those who have lived in several cultures and who can converse in at least two languages."

Daniel Meiland, Executive Chairman of Egon Zehnder International,
Harvard Business Review, 2003

"Two languages are better than one—for English language learners and for native-English speakers alike. Learning two (or more) languages is the hallmark of the educated person, and is encouraged in the academic circles of the college-bound high school student and in higher education."

Wayne P. Thomas and Virginia P. Collier, *School Effectiveness for Language Minority Students*

BILINGUAL PROGRAMS

"Education is one of society's most cost-effective investments . . . . To exclude from consideration genuine bilingual and multicultural programs, whose success has been demonstrated repeatedly, purely on the ideological grounds that they are 'un-American,' is irrational and simply panders to the neurotic paranoia of the patriotically correct (to borrow Robert Hughes's phrase)."

"Our societies urgently need more people with fluent bilingual skills, yet we demonize bilingual education, the only program capable of delivering bilingualism and biliteracy."

"Bilingual students who feel a sense of belonging in their classroom learning community are more likely to feel 'at home' in their society upon graduation and to contribute actively to building that society. Schools that have brought issues related to cultural and linguistic diversity from the periphery to the center of their mission are more likely to prepare students to thrive in the interdependent global society in which they will live."

Jim Cummins, *Negotiating Identities: Education for Empowerment in a Diverse Society*

"Bilingual education has the potential of being a transformative school practice, able to educate all children in ways that stimulate and expand their intellect and imagination, as they gain ways of expression and access different ways of being in the world."

Ofelia García, *Bilingual Education in the 21st Century: A Global Perspective*

CONFRONTING OUR DIFFERENCES

*"If nation-states are reimagined in more plural and inclusive ways,
there is potential for the recognition of not only greater political
democracy but greater ethnocultural and ethnolinguistic democracy as
well . . . . Ethnic and national conflicts are most often precipitated
when nation-states ignore demands for greater cultural and linguistic
democracy, not—as is commonly assumed—when they accommodate
them."*

Stephen May, *Language and Minority Rights*

*"As a nation built by immigrants, explorers, and exiles of many shores,
it is the ability to confront differences among its people that has led the
United States to achieve social advancements such as the abolition of
slavery, women's suffrage, civil rights legislation, and desegration."*

Elizabeth Pathy Salett, Diane R. Koslow, and Elsie Achugbue, *Race,
Ethnicity and Self: Identity in Multicultural Perspective*

BILINGUALISM IN THE U.S.

*"Bilingualism got a bad reputation, at least when it occurred among
the poor and downtrodden. By contrast, in jet-setters, fluency in many
languages has always been a sign of meritorious achievement and
prestige . . . . We believe that adding knowledge and skills is sound;
subtracting hard-earned capabilities—especially one as intrinsically
utilitarian as language fluency—is unsound."*

H. Ned Seelye and Jacqueline Howell Wasilewski, *Between Cultures:
Developing Self-Identity in a World of Diversity*

*"English-only policies fly in the face of the principles on which this
country was founded. Settlers came to America to escape the hierarchy
of Europe, to create a meritocracy where it didn't matter where your
parents came from, what they did for a living, what language they
spoke—all that mattered was what you did with your life, what you*

achieved, and how you treated your fellow citizens of the world. It is this principle that binds our nation together, not demands that we all speak the same language.

Daniel Ward, Editorial, *Language Magazine*, October 2008

"We all embrace English and accept its crucial importance in this country. But our country and our educational systems also have other needs—in science and in math, in history and in literature, in world consciousness and in world sensitivity. We desperately need competence in languages—and our huge and varied heritage language resources have a definite role to play in achieving such competence."

Joshua A. Fishman, "300-Plus Years of Heritage Language Education in the United States," in Joy Kreeft Peyton, Donald A. Ranard, and Scott McGinnis (Eds.), *Heritage Languages in America: Preserving a National Resource*

CHAPTER 9

From Puppet Shows to Bilingual Scrabble: 50 Activities to Enjoy with Your Kids at Home

SINGING

When you experience the enthusiasm and pride of a two-year-old singing the alphabet, it makes you want to teach him everything through songs! The repetition, the excitement, and the participation of parents or siblings make singing a great learning tool. Sing as often as you can. If you're struggling to remember the lyrics of classic songs from your childhood, you can find international CDs at the library or lyrics online. If your neighbors are away, you can also add musical instruments like a tam-tam, a guitar, a tambora, or a flute and turn the whole experience into a family talent show!

CAR PARTS

The goal is to include our heritage language in our daily activities, so we can help our children learn in seamless ways. On a warm and sunny day, when you're washing the car outside or fixing the brakes, why not include your children and expose them to a whole new set of vocabulary words? You can get a free bilingual technical dictionary in your heritage language when you purchase an auto or motorcycle repair manual in English from the well-known Haynes Publishing UK website. The dictionaries are available in seventeen languages. Very handy! Get your children their very own pair of coveralls and get your hands dirty together. If they switch to English, you can always spray them with the hose! (The experts agree: A sense of humor is a must in second-language acquisition.) Teach them the names of all the tools you're using. Go through the checklist in your owner's manual and help them locate the different car parts. Share stories about your first car, your dream car, and their dream cars. If you dread working on your car, now you can turn it into a learning experience and a great bonding time.

POSTCARD EXCHANGE

Before kids turn their backs on pen and paper completely, let them enjoy the thrills of getting a postcard in the mail with their name on it. Your children can create a chain with grandparents, cousins, aunts, and uncles. It's a fun way for kids to feel connected while practicing their reading *and* writing skills in the heritage language.

DECORATIONS

One of the fun outcomes of owning a home (I'm guessing!) is to have free reign with decorating and painting the walls. If you or someone in your family feels creative, you can write fun words all around the top border around the room or on one designated wall. (I had a friend in college who decorated her room with short poetry verses in Japanese, and it looked incredible!) You can also buy wooden letters and make up words; you can change them as the kids get older. We found a huge *Bonjour* wooden sign at a second-hand store one day, and it greets us every time we open the door. The girls and I are big fans of the painter Henri Matisse, so we have his name spelled out with some of his prints underneath and short words in French that describe them: *poisson*/fish, *rouge*/red, and *bateaux*/boats. You can also decorate their room with colorful posters with words in the heritage language. (Rolled up in a poster cardboard, they're light to mail.)

BILINGUAL BABYSITTERS

Many parents advise looking for a bilingual babysitter who can bring your native language into the house. Through your local university's message board or word of mouth from other parents, you can find qualified babysitters of all ages who speak your native language. If you find an older person who has lived in your home country, he or she may be able to share stories and anecdotes that can bring additional cultural knowledge to your children.

MUST READ!

If your child is in high school, I recommend getting a copy of *Coming of Age in a Globalized World: The Next Generation* by J. Michael Adams and Angelo Carfagna, published by Kumarian Press. It offers a concise explanation of globalization and explains why cultural awareness is key for today's students. As the authors explain, "To survive and succeed in this environment, individuals must understand the driving forces of globalization and the trends that will shape their lives as global citizens."

SESAME STREET AROUND THE WORLD

Although I try to play only French cartoons at home for the girls, I didn't want them to start kindergarten without the same cultural references as their American classmates, so I was excited to find *Sesame Street Around the World*. Children everywhere now recognize *Sesame Street* characters, as the show airs in many countries. *Sesame Street* promotes respect and cultural awareness by using characters children already know. As Rebecca Honig, a curriculum specialist at Sesame Workshop, explains, "Far, far away is a difficult concept for preschoolers. They are more connected to their own family and neighborhood, so that's where we started. We knew we had to take what's familiar and apply it to the rest of the world." Check out the website for fun videos, including Global Grover doing a Russian dance! www.sesamework shop.org/aroundtheworld and www.sesameworkshop.org/initiatives/respect

BILINGUAL NEWSPAPERS

Subscribe to a bilingual newspaper or one published solely in your heritage language. You can also ask the editorial staff if they know of other print resources in your area. Or contact your nearest consulate or your local librarian.

GARDENING

There is a small patch of dirt in our backyard that I keep trying to turn into a beautiful vegetable garden. Natasha and Sofiya, luckily, are not too demanding, so we end up having a great time, planting, watering, removing weeds, and watching carrots and radishes grow. The herb garden on the windowsill is our next project. There are so many great lessons to be learned from gardening (in the heritage language, of course!) with small children, as well as some technical words you might not use every day. Kids learn about the tools they need, the soil, the seasons, the weather, and how to care for different plants and flowers.

READING

We all know reading is important, but many of us, I'll venture to say, still aren't reading enough. And for many parents and children, unfortunately, access to books is still a luxury. It's only when I explored the research on reading and the statistics that I truly understood the power of reading and how it can change a child's life. And children who read or are read to regularly in their heritage language will develop a richer vocabulary. Now it's almost impossible to say no to the girls when they ask me for one more story at bedtime!

"BEING BILINGUAL" ESSAY CONTEST

The National Association for Bilingual Education organizes an annual writing contest for bilingual students in grades 3 to 5, 6 to 8, and 9 to 11. The winners in each category get their essays published in NABE's conference catalog, which is distributed to more than 3,000 people, and an all-expense paid trip with one parent to the annual conference. Your children can read the entries of past winners and get inspired to share their thoughts on growing up bilingual. Encourage your children to send in their submissions. You can also check out other contests sponsored by NABE, including nominating your favorite "Bilingual Teacher of the Year."

WORD ORIGINS

If you have a particularly inquisitive child, or just a knack for making everything sound interesting, there is something to be said for studying word origins to better understand the structure of a language. Webster's *Third New International Dictionary* offers more than

140,000 entries describing word origins. You can request the dictionary at your local library.

SATELLITE TELEVISION

I always look forward to a visit at my friend Inna's house because
there's a good chance the Russian channel will be on for her elderly
mother, and although I struggle to understand it all, it sounds wonderful! Nowadays, you can get television stations in almost any language. It's all to be used in moderation, but for older children it's a fun
way to keep in touch with the news, pop culture, or anything the family is interested in. Younger children will enjoy cartoons in the heritage language. You can also get broadcasts online. A good site to help
you search the channel that's right for you is http://dir.yahoo.com/
News_and_Media/Television/Stations/By_Region/Countries/. You
can also check out BeelineTV and wwiTV for more networks. As one
parent I know advises, "Let your children watch television ONLY in
the heritage language!"

OUR GLOBAL GOVERNMENT

I think many of us who have multicultural families are particularly
pleased to see a more diverse government leading the nation. The day
after the inauguration of President Obama, the *Boston Globe* published a front-page article describing the families of the President and
First Lady Michelle Obama as black, white, Asian, Christian, Muslim,
and Jewish. Their extended families combined speak nine languages,
including English, Indonesian, French, Cantonese, German, Hebrew,
Swahili, Luo and Igbo. But looking past the First Family, there are also
many government officials who were raised outside of the U.S. who
bring an international perspective to their work. If you have an older
child who's interested in politics, you can research this information
online and bring to light the cultural and linguistic backgrounds of

today's U.S. government. A member of the organization Families in Global Transition, Ann Cottrell, was kind enough to share some of her findings:

1. Valerie Jarrette, senior advisor, was born in Iran and moved to the U.K. during her childhood.
2. James Jones, national security adviser, grew up in France.
3. Tim Geithner, treasury secretary, spent his childhood years in Zimbabwe, India, and Thailand.
4. Scott Gration, policy advisor, grew up in the Congo.

VOICE RECORDERS

Natasha and Sofiya love listening to themselves on the recorder, as most children do. It's a great way to get them talking (and, if you want, you can make subtle corrections in their pronunciation). You can also download the dialogue onto your computer if you want to save some particularly funny conversations! I also secretly tape them sometimes during dinner, which they find hilarious later on. Those recordings serve me well too, to stop them from crying during a temper tantrum. I press "play" and they're so surprised to hear their voices that they forget what they were crying about!

A WELL-STOCKED IPOD

I'll admit it: I still have a Walkman. But I realize the wide-ranging benefits of using iPods, especially when you can easily download material in your native language. Podcasts and music from your home country are great ways to keep kids (especially teens) happy and in touch with the latest cultural trends. To sustain a first (or second) language, you need motivation and a reason to use it, so if you keep your children's iPods loaded in the heritage language, they will be well on their way!

WANT TO WATCH A VIDEO?

I've been told that when it comes to teenagers, the opinions and testimonies of complete strangers can sometimes have more impact than their own parents' point of view. The Highline School District in Seattle, Washington, must have heard about this. With more than 18,000 enrolled students who speak more than eighty languages, the school district decided to put together a seven-DVD set that focuses on the lives of successful bilingual professionals. The series is called *Speak Your Languages* and can be requested through your library. It is invaluable for teenagers to understand that learning two languages will have huge consequences on their personal and professional lives.

LAUNDRY DAY

I decided a while back that I would include my children in my daily chores around the house because it automatically turns the work into fun! I'm trying to soak up the girls' enthusiasm for cleaning activities that adults usually see as annoyances. Involving small children on laundry day usually requires more patience, but I think it's well worth it. I'm amazed at how many vocabulary words they've learned from this activity. We sort the colors before the wash, and then we divide the clothes when we put them away in the closet and drawers. Repetition is key in language development, and this is one activity we *need* to repeat, whether we want to or not!

SCRABBLE

Dr. Jean-Marc Dewaele, a well-known researcher on trilingualism, once said in an interview that he likes to play Scrabble with his daughter, who speaks English, Dutch, and French. If they can do it with three languages, we should be able to handle bilingual Scrabble! The game is now offered in twenty-nine languages. There's even a game called My First Scrabble, for children three to six years old, and Scrabble

Junior, for five- to ten-year-olds. When it comes to word games, Scrabble is the best known, but there are countless others (remember Boggle?) that can bring the family together. You can play in the heritage language only or enjoy the benefits of bilingualism and play in both languages.

If you prefer, Monopoly is also a great board game to play as a family, and it is now available in twenty-seven languages. Most international editions use the country's currency and specific cultural sites, which makes the game even more educational.

FIESTA AT HOME!

I love activities that involve eating. Parents who have organized fiestas with their children rave about it. It's not so much about the food, really; it's more about the atmosphere you create around the meal. First, choose a traditional dish for dinner. Then ask everyone to come to the table dressed in "culturally appropriate" fashion, which can mean a kimono or a traditional Russian silk dress, depending on your background. Take a picture of the whole family at the table, and then let the children direct the conversation—in the heritage language, of course. If you're lucky to have relatives living nearby, invite them over. Add decorations and background music, and watch your children enjoy this memorable, authentic evening.

You can also celebrate a cultural holiday from a different country to expose your children to other traditions. Learn as a family: do some background research together at the library or ask well-placed neighbors or coworkers. Then guide your children through the bright colors and delicious flavors of other cultures.

POETRY NIGHT

One important benefit of being bilingual is enjoying the literature of both cultures and glimpsing different lifestyles, behaviors, and beliefs.

In many cultures, poetry is a central part of people's lives. If you have creative souls in your house, you can organize your own poetry recital for the family. Each member has to choose one poem in the heritage language, learn it by heart, and present it on Poetry Night. I recommend making a video of their performances! Children can also write their own poetry, which can be saved in a special family book. Learning to read, memorize, and recite poetry helps children become more sensitive to the particular techniques and forms of their heritage language. This activity can start with simple poetry and develop into more complex pieces as children get older.

WHERE DOES THAT PIECE GO?

This activity is great for a rainy day or when your child is sick. Find a puzzle of a landmark from your country, and sit down together to tackle it. If you can't find the right puzzle, either in stores or online, some companies will make a puzzle directly from a photo. If you both have visited the site, you can share memories of your trip, or you can talk about the history of the landmark and its cultural relevance. This activity not only gets your child to practice her heritage language with you and find out something about her culture, but it also teaches patience and teamwork!

MAP IT!

Put a map on the wall and let your children mark each town or country they've traveled to. Help them find where their parents were born and where they were born. You can also put pictures of relatives over the areas where they live. You can mark all the countries around the world where people speak your heritage language, to show your children the value of learning to speak it. Each time you look at the map, you can focus on a different theme, such as international landmarks, indigenous animals, or national sports. Think about your children's hobbies and interests and try to find a way to give them an international angle. For example, if they like soccer, try to locate the birthplace of the most famous soccer players around the world!

PUT ON A PUPPET SHOW

A puppet show brings the family together and lets everyone participate at their own language level. If the parents put on the show, they can recount stories that expose the cultural values they want to pass on to their children. When the kids put on the puppet show, they practice their storytelling skills in their heritage language in a creative and collaborative way. Children can make their own puppets and decorate them with traditional clothing. They can use favorite storylines from books they've read, to guide them along. Putting on a puppet show takes some effort and preparation, but it's guaranteed fun for the whole family. (And as with most of these activities, there are many variations, depending on how much time and resources you can commit and how creative the family feels!)

DICTATION CAN BE FUN! (REALLY!)

Some parents might cringe when they think back on this "old-fashioned" teaching strategy, but before you dismiss it, try it with your children. It can be a calming exercise for restless kids. As an ESL student, I loved dictations. I felt much more in control than I did when I had to speak. Writing skills in the heritage language often are overlooked, but they open up a whole new world. How you approach this exercise will make all the difference. Let your children choose a beautiful pen and notebook, let them decorate their desks, give them lots of praise, and keep the mood light and stress-free. Depending on their learning style and personality, your children might just take to it!

GET AN AUTOGRAPH

Request a signed photo of your child's favorite bilingual singer, actor, or athlete that reads "I'm proud you're learning Spanish!" or any other heritage language. On the book's website (www.bilingualby choice.com) I include a list of famous bilingual artists and what languages they speak. You often can make contact either through their talent agency, the television shows on which they appear, or other business ventures in which they're involved, such as restaurants. You can also try the website www.fanmail.biz.

FOCUS ON HOBBIES

Here's a common piece of advice from parents who've succeeded in raising bilingual children past those tricky years where English seems to take over: Focus on the children's favorite interests and hobbies. For a while, let the conversation in the heritage language revolve around subjects your kids are passionate about. Look up some of the top people in those fields who are from your native country, print biographies and interesting facts and pictures, find books online, and read together. The topic will keep them interested and make them more knowledgeable in their cultural heritage.

ART WEAR

Let your child choose a cool or common saying in the heritage language; then put it on a T-shirt. Some online sites will let you design your own T-shirt at a reasonable cost. (Try the keywords "T-shirt design.")

HARRY POTTER GOES GLOBAL

If your children loved reading the Harry Potter books in English, you should know that these bestsellers are now available in more than sixty languages! Read with them during some quality one-on-one time and learn a few new vocabulary words together!

CULTURE FOR KIDS

Two great sources for bilingual books are the catalogs Culture for Kids and Asia for Kids. You'll find multicultural crafts and activities, books, CDs, DVDs, dictionaries, toys, flashcards, stickers, and more. I think I'm going to give my friends and every member of my family a catalog; when birthdays and holidays come around, they will know just what to get Natasha and Sofiya!

INTERNATIONAL PETS

One mom bought her daughter a Chihuahua and told her the dog could only learn commands in Spanish! The daughter trained her puppy and now reads Spanish stories to him before bedtime! Of course, adopting a pet isn't something to be taken lightly, but if you're planning on doing so anyway, you may as well make him or her monolingual in your heritage language!

STICKER MANIA

Some parents increase their children's interest in the heritage language by covering their house in stickers! They put a sticker on almost every household object and make language learning fun again.

LITERATE PLACEMATS

It's fairly easy to draw or cut out new vocabulary words, glue them on a posterboard, and laminate it to make learning placemats! Or the arts and crafts–challenged (like me) can have someone back home buy placemats and send or bring them to you. They're light, and they don't take up any space in a suitcase! You can also buy cups, bowls, and silverware with fun printed vocabulary words. Sometimes we take one word and make up little stories during mealtime. I wish I had recorded some of those early improvisations. Half the time, Natasha and Sofiya are having so much fun that they don't even realize they're eating a plateful of green beans!

HOST AN INTERNATIONAL STUDENT

When you're unable to travel back to your home country, a great way to bring first hand cultural insights into your home is to host an international student for a few weeks. There are different organizations that you can search online and contact directly or through your child's school. Obviously, the student you're hosting is here to learn English. But you'll find opportunities for everyone to speak the heritage language. For example, you can use the One Language One Environment strategy during down time after school. Your visiting student will feel less homesick as she adjusts to her new surroundings.

Another possibility is to invite a dear cousin or close friend that your child particularly misses to stay with you during the summer months. It's a great cultural experience for everyone involved!

SCAVENGER HUNT

In our house this activity starts with two excited little girls waiting for instructions, holding their Dora the Explorer backpacks! We hide five to ten items around the house for them to find. The clues are written out on cards, which we read out to them. We try to use new vocabulary words mixed with expressions they already understand. As they fill up their backpacks, we keep the dialogue going as we move around the house, focusing on opposites, colors, objects, and the furniture in different rooms. The game has many variations, and parents can make the clues as simple or as complex as they want, depending on the children's language level. To practice numbers, young children have to count steps to go from one hidden object to the next.

MEMORY BINGO

This classic game reinforces vocabulary through repetition that the whole family can play together. With a bag full of picture cards, it also travels well to restaurants, airplanes, and anywhere there's waiting involved. You can make your own cards to update the vocabulary words as your children progress in the language, or you can purchase one of the many games on the market.

BILINGUAL DOLLS

Next time relatives ask you what they can get for your child's birthday, let them know about the Language Littles' adorable bilingual dolls. Big and small, they speak between twenty-five and thirty phrases in Spanish, French, German, Italian, Greek, Russian, Japanese, Chinese, Hebrew, or Korean. The company's website also offers fun multilingual games and coloring pages to print. All dolls come with a six-month warranty. Also, there are more and more choices on the market for bilingual Spanish/English dolls.

SIDEWALK ART

With a bucket of thick colored chalk, you and your children can practice new words and numbers by drawing on the driveway or on the sidewalk. It's a fun and easy way to practice spelling or counting. Go to http://www.crayola.com/outdoor/index.cfm and find outdoor games to play with chalk. They even sell 3-D sidewalk chalk now; you wear 3-D glasses to look at your artwork!

DVDS FROM AROUND THE WORLD

Many families suggest buying a universal DVD player to keep the selection of movies more varied, especially for older children as they develop their preferences and interests. I respect what the American

Association of Pediatrics says about the negative effects of television on younger children, but as a mom of multiples I will admit that I more than once put my babies in front of a twenty-minute Baby Einstein DVD (which has a French version), in exchange for a hot shower! As Natasha and Sofiya got older, we ended up watching them together to repeat all the new vocabulary words, and also because they're very soothing, even for adults!

THE TRAVEL CHANNEL

Armchair travelers can still practice their language skills! The Travel Channel is a great way for children and adults to explore the world. Look up the programming ahead of time, research the country, get books at the library, and pretend you're planning a trip. You can cover vocabulary for packing clothes, seasons, famous landmarks, food, cultural etiquette, et cetera. You can adapt the information depending on your children's ages. The idea is to watch together, interact, and learn about new places.

READ UP ON ELECTRONICS

I know some people don't like to read instructions when they buy new electronics equipment. But for the sake of language learning, the next time you bring home a new blender or a washing machine, take a closer look at the manual. There are often dozens of languages represented; with a little bit of creativity, you will find yourself with a new set of vocabulary words to teach! Pretend you can't read the small type without your glasses, and ask your child to help you with it! Get your hands on manuals for the television, video camera, DVD player, or iPod. If you're a parent who speaks French or Spanish, you've probably noticed that almost every thing you buy, from shampoo to diapers, has a description in your language. On the next rainy day, go through the house with your children and try to spot all the multilingual objects! The last time I was in France, I was stunned to see that a child's sweater I bought had a tag with washing instructions in sixteen languages! How fun is that? (Slightly itchy, too!)

Online Activities

INTERNET RADIO

There are stations from virtually every country at your fingertips and you can access most of them for free. Sites like www.live-radio.net will help you locate the right one, or you can access www.xmradio.com.

Some radio stations are designed for young listeners with songs and nursery rhymes they can sing along to. Older children can keep up with the latest pop culture music in the parents' home country. We play French music often in our house and my daughters are avid singers. Very often the lyrics include new words that we don't use in our every day conversations. As you know, children learn well through repetition and having fun, which makes this activity a must!

YOUTUBE

The day I found five-minute-long T'choupi cartoons on the website YouTube.com was a happy day at our house! Natasha and Sofiya had discovered the French cartoon character through books, but to see him on the computer screen, talking and getting into all sorts of trouble, got them really excited. You can play each episode separately, or you can make playlists so your kids can watch a few in a row, if you need more time in the kitchen! With some preplanning and pre-screening, it's amazing what you'll find on this site for your children, from songs and cartoons to cultural dance recitals and music videos. Anything and everything. Look for the YouTube handbook at the bottom of the main page to find tips on how to use the site. It's definitely a supervised activity, but it has great potential.

FREE ONLINE LANGUAGE COURSES

The British Broadcasting Corporation (BBC) offers free twelve-week online courses for beginners in French, German, Spanish, Italian, Chinese, Portuguese, and Greek at www.bbc.co.uk/languages. You can use the site to supplement your children's exposure to the language. They even get a certificate at the end when they finish the course! The site provides a "quick-fix" section with twelve "essential holiday phrases" in thirty-six languages, as well as language tests, dictionaries, and learning games.

Children are invited to share their thoughts or personal anecdotes about their language experience in a section called "Your Say." Most children will have a great feeling of pride and accomplishment when they see their words on a website such as the BBC's.

You also can search the keywords "free online language classes" to find other options. For example, you can access free German courses on Deutsche Welle's website at www.dw-world.de/germancourses.

CURRENT EVENTS

When your children are old enough to read and be interested in international news, check out www.bbc.co.uk, which now offers its news program in thirty-four languages, complete with audio. If you or your teenage children want to perfect your English, there is also an extensive BBC Learning English section (www.bbc.co.uk/worldservice/learning english) with exercises, vocabulary, grammar, stories, interactive games, and more. You'll soon be able to imitate a great British accent!

XIHALIFE

The new multilingual social network Xihalife, at www.xihalife.com, is "targeted at people living outside their home country, as well as multilingual people around the world." People from different language and cultural backgrounds can share their blogs and music, and play games with other young adults. The founders of Xihalife write, "Our language recognition and filtering technology enables users to select not only one, but several different languages to communicate with new friends and people they care about." XIIIA, by the way, means "fun" or "happy" in Mandarin, as well as "hip-hop" in Cantonese!

CHAT GROUPS

Keep connected with other parents who are raising bilingual children by networking on language and cultural sites. At the popular www.cafemom.com there are more than 250 clubs under the heading Cultures and Ethnicity, many of them divided by specific language groups. At www.polishforums.com, you can post questions and start conversations about all things Polish, from recipes to grammar rules. To find motivation and support from other parents who are raising bilingual children, I recommend the Yahoo group Multicultural Munchkins.

INTERNATIONAL RESEARCH ON BILINGUALISM

You can find a great deal of international research on bilingualism, if you would like to read about the subject in your native language. If you have concerns or questions about raising a deaf child with a second language, for example, I would recommend Francois Grosjean's research, which is now available in thirty-one languages on his site at www.francoisgrosjean.ch/the_right_en.html.

THE INTERNET INTERNATIONALIZED!

In 2008, the Internet Corporation for Assigned Names and Numbers (ICANN) removed the restriction to use only Roman characters in website addresses. Considering that ninety-two percent of the world's people live in countries where English is not the native language, it seems like a reasonable move. This ruling, once the complications have been ironed out, will have a huge impact on Internet users who do not speak English or other Latin-based languages. For example, the Russian Internet community will soon be able to create Cyrillic domain names when building a website. According to Brenda Danet and Susan Herring, editors of *The Multilingual Internet*, two-thirds of Internet users live in Europe and Asia. Stay tuned for more Internet content in your heritage language!

The panelists at the 2008 Internet Governance Forum, held in India, also found that more languages need to be represented. In a session titled "Reaching the Next Billion: Access and Multilingualism," the experts agreed that "Content in local languages is as essential as connectivity. People must be able to create and receive information in their local language and to be able to express themselves in ways their peers can understand." (Retrieved from http://portal.unesco.org/ci/en/ev.php-URL_ID=27869&URL_DO=DO_TOPIC&URL_SECTION=201.html.)

SKYPE

Once you start using Skype with a webcam to communicate with relatives far away, you will wonder how you ever lived without it! We rarely use the phone with our families anymore. I encourage parents (including my oldest sister Brigitte!) to sign up, and don't put it off another day. Life is busy, but time is passing by and cousins are missing out on valuable face-to-face talks and giggles. I wish we had had this kind of technology in 1982 when we relocated to the U.S., instead of losing touch with most of my extended family. It's free and takes two minutes to download, so there's no excuse!

CHAPTER 10

From Bilingual Storytime to Kids' Language Clubs: 50 Activities in Your Local Community

MATISSE OR PICASSO?

It's important to look for variety in our activities to help children build their vocabulary in the heritage language. A visit to an art museum gives the family a chance to step out of their daily routine and open up new worlds. There are more than 1,300 art museums around the country that exhibit classic art works, contemporary art, textiles, furniture, musical instruments, sculptures, drawings, and photographs. Many museums offer free admission at least one day a week or accept donations.

The Museum of Fine Arts in Boston, for example, offers free admission to children ages seven to seventeen every weekday after three p.m. and on weekends. There are free guided tours in French, Spanish, and Russian. Gallery talks, which focus on a particular exhibit, are given in Spanish, Russian, French, and American Sign Language.

Children can discuss the subject matter, the colors, the lighting. They can describe their favorite piece and explain what makes it special. With some background research, parents can share anecdotes about the lives of the artists, the locations depicted in the paintings, or the history of the specific art period.

WHAT LANGUAGES ARE THE NEIGHBORS SPEAKING?

The Modern Language Association provides a great tool on its website that lets you search what languages families are speaking in your neighborhood. When you access the website at www.mla.org/map_data, you can enter your state and your county, and it will show you the percentage of people over age five who speak a language other than English at home. For example, in Rockingham County, New Hampshire, where we live, 4,550 people speak French at home. You'll be amazed at how many languages are spoken in your neighborhood and stunned at why we're still calling this country monolingual!

With this information, parents can promote language clubs for kids in their communities. All it takes to start is a few flyers at the library, grocery store, and local churches. The meetings can take place weekly or biweekly, at a park, a community center, or at someone's home. Like regular playdates, language clubs can be organized in any number of ways, but the one rule that must stick is that only the heritage language can be spoken!

Language clubs allow children to forge meaningful friendships with other native speakers, but they can also include children enrolled in foreign language classes who want to practice their skills.

HOUSES OF WORSHIP

Churches around the country offer services in different languages, including French, Polish, Italian, Indonesian, and many more. Many churches also organize social gatherings after mass. One mother from Washington, D.C., decided to attend an Italian church coffee hour every Sunday with her son, who happily displayed his language skills in front of the older parishioners, who were quick to encourage him in his progress. In this situation, children get a chance to hear people, outside of their family, speak their heritage language in a laid-back and friendly environment. If there are sweets being passed around, your child might even encourage you to make it a weekly outing!

SISTER CITIES

Sister Cities International is a nonprofit organization that brings together U.S. and international cities to increase global awareness, improve business developments, and exchange ideas in different fields including technology and the arts. You can find a directory on their website at www.sister-cities.org/icrc/directory/index to see if your city has an international "sister city." Many communities organize cultural events and exchanges, giving families a chance to practice their language skills with other natives, as well as spreading cultural awareness in the community. The Sister Cities website allows you to search your city and offers links to cultural programs in your area and contact information for your local "sister cities" chapter.

For example, Asheville, North Carolina, has six sister cities: San Cristobal de las Casas and Valladolid in Mexico, Vladikavkaz in Russia, Karpenisi in Greece, and Saumur in France. Asheville has welcomed international musicians, journalists, jewelers, culinary students, basketball players, among other guests.

Although not all languages will be represented at these cultural events, it's also possible for a community to request a sister city in a particular country or to search through the existing list of international cities looking to make a connection with U.S. sister cities.

STORYTIME AT THE LIBRARY

If we read with our children in our heritage language on a daily basis, their vocabulary will drastically increase and their imaginations will soar. One important resource is, of course, the library. Through the interloan library system, you can request books or CDs, and your library will search larger libraries for your items. Many libraries also offer weekly or monthly bilingual storytimes for school-age children. If none exist at your library, you may be able to start your own! After you approach the librarian with your idea, you can put a flyer up at the front desk to see if there are a few families who would be interested in signing up. If you are unable to host it yourself, you can contact a school teacher, a relative, or an elderly volunteer in your community who can host the half-hour or forty-five-minute sessions. Bilingual storytime programs can mix storytelling, puppet shows, music and sing-alongs, poetry, craft activities, and much more.

English-speaking families will be interested to join as well, to expose their children to another language. Most parents with young children, bilingual or not, are always looking for fun outings that will get them out of the house!

At the seventeen library locations in San Jose, California, for example, there are bilingual programs in a number of languages, including Japanese, Tagalog, Spanish, Vietnamese, Chinese, and Hindi. Smaller libraries, in towns such as Leesburg, Florida, with 20,000 inhabitants, are also quick to add bilingual story time to their schedule when they are approached by enthusiastic families in the community.

A TRIP TO THE UNITED NATIONS

A tour of the United Nations in New York City can send a powerful message to children. The lecture tours are available in more than twenty-five languages. Your children will learn about the history of the U.N., the contributions of peacekeepers around the world, and how the Security Council works. There is also a great bookstore with a kids section and a post-office where children can send a postcard to relatives with a special U.N. stamp on it. The United Nations News website also offers international news in forty-four languages. If you can't travel to New York, find out if your child's school organizes (or will organize!) a Model U.N. session where children play the role of delegates from different countries working through real-life negotiations, which can be an eye-opening experience!

CONTACT YOUR CONSULATE

Consulates and embassies around the country organize cultural events for the community throughout the year. It's a chance to meet other native speakers and find out about local resources. The website, www.embassyworld.com/Foreign_Embassies_In_The_USA/ Embassies_To_USA.html, will let you search the contact information to your closest embassy or general consulate.

For example, the Netherlands Consulate General in Miami, Florida, provides a list of Dutch events throughout the U.S. The information, written in Dutch, is posted at www.sica.nl. The site also gives you a link to Radio Netherlands to learn about political events. For younger children, there is another link at www.discoverthenetherlands .org that helps students understand the country's culture and gives them a forum to share their own stories about the Netherlands.

THE MENU, PLEASE!

Next time you treat yourself to a nice family dinner out, look for a restaurant whose owner or staff speak your heritage language and let your children do the talking! You can read the menu together, discuss dishes and their ingredients, and describe the flavors and spices. It's inevitable that the conversation will soon include stories from your own childhood, brought on by the delicious aromas around the table.

FREE MOVIES AT THE UNIVERSITY

If a nearby university has a foreign language program, find out if they have a foreign film series. In many language programs, students watch films for class credit, but the theater is generally open to the general public as well. I belong to a French group that takes advantages of the screenings at the University of New Hampshire. These artistic films can help your (older) children gain some insights into their cultural background, learn new vocabulary, and help start engaging conversations at home afterwards.

At Southeast Missouri State University, for example, the Foreign Languages Department shows around thirty films each semester in French, German, and Spanish that are free and open to the public.

SUMMER LANGUAGE CAMP

Most children treasure the experience of going to summer camp. It's another great way for parents to make language learning fun! You can search online to see if there are any existing language camps in your region. Some organizations also offer study abroad and international camps.

For example, Concordia Language Villages in Minnesota offers summer camp programs in more than fifteen languages for children seven to eighteen years old. The culturally authentic villages, where the children live, are scattered throughout the state, as well as in Savannah, Georgia.

TRIPS TO YOUR HOMELAND

A well-timed trip to your native country—say, when your child starts to praise the virtues of English-only!—can make all the difference in his heritage language skills. It's especially useful if your relatives back home do not speak English, or promise to restrain from speaking it! Many parents I spoke with offered the advice of a trip as a way to cement a child's motivation and sense of purpose in learning a heritage language fluently, particularly when long-lasting relationships with cousins and friends are forged.

THE LOCAL GROCERY STORE

Many neighborhoods in larger cities still have small grocery stores run by immigrant families. You can take the kids along, introduce them to the shopkeeper, and find some special treats that cannot be found in regular grocery stores. If you can't find a store where your heritage language is spoken, there are still significant benefits to shopping at an ethnic grocery store. We met a Cambodian shopkeeper who owns Lo's Seafood & Asian Market in Portsmouth, NH, who has introduced us to the local flavors and made us more aware of what my sister and her children are feasting on in Phnom-Penh. He speaks Khmer, French, and English fluently. These outings make children feel part of the community and help them understand that speaking a second language is common, and an invaluable way to connect with other people.

THE COW FLEW OVER THE MOON

This activity explores a whole new set of vocabulary words. All you have to do is pitch a tent in the backyard, get your hands on binoculars or a telescope, and enjoy a night sky viewing together. Choose a night when the sky is clear and the moon is visible. Free star charts are available online; they'll help you locate specific stars and constellations. Watch for satellites, the craters on the moon, the Milky Way, or a shooting star. You can talk about the solar system, the space program, the last shuttle mission and what it accomplished, or if there really are aliens out there! Learning new vocabulary words is easier when it doesn't feel like homework, and if you can provide an added bonus like roasted marshmallows (made in the kitchen beforehand if you don't want to risk the backyard bonfire!) you might find yourself with a new favorite family activity.

BEHIND THE SCENES AT THE OLYMPICS

If your child has favorite Olympic athletes who speak your heritage language, you can get into the Olympic spirit by assisting their training sessions at three different U.S. Olympic Training Centers in Chula Vista, California; Lake Placid, New York; and Colorado Springs, Colorado. You can sign up for a guided tour and watch them train for free. School group tours are also available.

One family also shared another well-received family outing that the children talked about for months afterwards. They organized a behind-the-scenes tour of a baseball stadium and asked a local volunteer (found through the local university's foreign language department) to do the tour in their heritage language.

TRADING SPACES

If you feel comfortable trading your home with someone else in a country where they speak your heritage language, you will have the chance to practice the language and visit the sights to give your children firsthand exposure to the culture. At www.HomeExchange.com the process is as simple as 1) pick a country, 2) find a listing, and 3) contact a member. According to the travel expert Arthur Frommer, "Home exchange is the single most logical, sensible, economical, and rewarding method of travel." It takes a bit of faith to jump in but if you take the time to research well, you might be happy to do it every year! There are different sites that you can explore online by just using "International Home Exchange" as your keywords. Make sure you have all your questions answered before you embark on your new adventure.

GLOBAL GREETERS

This is a great concept! In 1992, a group of volunteers started the Global Greeter Network in New York City to give free guided tours (with a strict no-tipping policy) to visitors and show off their city. The idea was so well received that they now have volunteers who have joined the network in such varied destinations as Houston, Texas; Buenos Aires, Argentina; Melbourne, Australia; Nantes, France; and The Hague, in the Netherlands. If you're not visiting a country where they speak your heritage language, you can always try to get a volunteer who does. The flexibility of a personalized guided tour is always welcome when you have small, unpredictable children!

DON'T FEED THE MONKEYS!

When you're practicing your heritage language with your children at a zoo, as they check out the tigers, there's a good chance it won't feel like homework! They will be so excited that they won't even realize they're not using English. Find out if the zoo hires volunteers to give guided tours and if they offer them in your heritage language. If not, a few minutes of research on the Internet, to find interesting facts about the animals you will see, will easily qualify you to do the tour yourself! From discussing the animals' feeding habits to habitats, you're guaranteed a long list of new vocabulary words! When planning your trip, don't forget that many zoos have a donation policy at least one day a week so check ahead of time. For some of its special attractions, the Bronx Zoo even drops its prices when the temperature drops. You can also sometimes get a discount when you arrive closer to closing time.

A VISIT TO THE FIRE STATION

Most fire stations offer public tours; with a couple of phone calls, you might be able to locate a firefighter who speaks your heritage language.

(And for this or any other community activity, don't forget you can always contact your city's visitors center or Chamber of Commerce or your local university's foreign-language department to locate volunteers who can give your family a tour in your language.) At the fire station, your children will be able to climb in the fire engine, see the equipment they use, and find out about the work itself.

Some cities along the coast also offer tours of their fireboats. If you can't do the tour in your language, do it in English; then, when you're home, you can find a virtual tour online (keywords: Fire Station Virtual Tours) and provide the commentary in your heritage language!

CHILDREN'S MUSEUM

Check out your local Children's Museum to see if they offer special multicultural activities and find out how you can make one happen! The Children's Museum of Indianapolis, for example, offers information on its website in Spanish, German, French, Russian, Chinese, and Japanese. One of its galleries on-site focuses on foreign cultures. Approach the staff at your local museum to organize an international festival that educates the public on your native country. Activities can include a fun language lesson with your children as proud teachers!

COLLEGE AND UNIVERSITY RESOURCES

You can find a wealth of information through your local university's foreign-language department: lectures and activities, films, and young students eager to practice their language skills. Many universities provide a listing of multicultural resources (with contact information) available in the community, including newspapers and magazines, grocers, places of worship, and cultural organizations. Universities also have international friendship groups made up of members of the community—young and old—who welcome and assist new international students arriving on campus. It's a great way to meet other parents who are raising bilingual children, as well as students who will be happy to hear a familiar accent.

FAMILIES FIRST

This nonprofit organization reaches out to parents from different cultural and socioeconomic backgrounds through parental workshops, lectures, and playgroups for children of all ages. It's also a good way to meet parents who have recently relocated to the U.S. If you're thinking about starting a bilingual or multilingual playgroup, or you just want to get in touch with other international families, this is the place to visit. Through Families First in Portsmouth, I met parents who were raising their children with Spanish, Russian, and Indonesian. Even if your language is not represented, it's always helpful to show our children that growing up with two languages is quite common.

A CITY TOUR

Gather a group of friends who speak your heritage language or who want to practice it, and contact your local Chamber of Commerce or Visitors Center and ask for a guided tour of your town in your heritage language. You can keep it short and fun by targeting sites that will entertain your children, depending on their ages.

Also, every major city offers bus tours in different languages to welcome visitors and give them a glimpse of all the attractions and landmarks that make the city unique. Travel to the nearest big city and act like a tourist!

Cities offer countless other resources for maintaining a second language. Buy a membership to your favorite museum and visit regularly. Find out about specialized bookstores, music stores, ethnic neighborhoods and restaurants, church services, and fun, kid-friendly attractions. Grab every pamphlet that's written in different languages and go over the vocabulary at home. Every time you travel to a new city, get on the trolley and give your children the chance to expand their vocabulary *and* get a great U.S. history lesson!

MULTICULTURAL EVENTS

Although some people would still like to believe we're all white and Protestant, many more are ready to celebrate this country's multiculturalism. And you don't have to live in a big city to participate. For example, in Laconia, New Hampshire, a town of 16,000 people, the city council organizes an annual Multicultural Market Day event in September for "celebrating diversity and world cultures." The town wholeheartedly celebrates the more than thirty countries represented in its immigrant and refugee population. The festival of cultural arts and crafts attracts close to 5,000 visitors every year. Attending a multicultural event is just one way to teach our children to respect and appreciate diversity.

TOURIST LANDMARKS

While researching this book, I contacted more than a hundred visitors centers around the country, and I'm happy to report that more and more tour companies, organizations, and cultural landmarks are looking for ways to reach out to non-English speaking visitors. Before you travel to a new vacation spot, find out about activities that are available in your heritage language. You can contact the city's visitors center, the International Women's Club, the Newcomer's Club, the local university's foreign-language department, or a cultural organization to give you some ideas and references.

For example, in historic Philadelphia, you can tour the city with a guide dressed as Ben Franklin and "learn about the history, stories and significance behind the nation's most treasured landmarks," with tours available in Spanish, French, Italian, German, and American Sign Language.

At the Grand Canyon National Park in Nevada, you can now learn about the geology and history of this national treasure in six different languages, including Japanese. The GPS Ranger tours, as they're called, are self-paced and "delivered through the GPS Ranger™, a patent-pending, handheld computer device that delivers compelling video, audio, musical soundtrack and historical photography based on the location of the user through the power of GPS (Global Positioning System) technology."

At Cape Canaveral in Florida, you can visit the Kennedy Space Center and learn more about NASA's space missions, past and present, including the International Space Station Center, the LC 39 Observation Gantry, and the Apollo/Saturn V Center. Site maps, audio tours, and books are available in French, German, Italian, Portuguese, Spanish, and Japanese. Bon voyage!

CULTURAL ORGANIZATIONS

When I contacted the Chamber of Commerce in Manchester, New Hampshire to find out about French-language resources in the city, they told me about the Franco-American Center that offers cinema nights, French classes, photography exhibits, a well-stocked library, and lots more. Through these kinds of cultural organizations around the country, you can get your hands on books, magazines, and newspapers and find out about local events that can put you in touch with other families who speak your heritage language. The staff will most likely be very helpful in finding you the right resources when you tell them you're raising bilingual children. For example, they may help locate a pen pal for your children. At a certain age, peers who share the same language and cultural background can encourage our children in their language development and often have more influence than parents do.

POETRY CONTESTS

Many language organizations or teachers' associations, such as the American Association of Teachers of Slavic and Eastern European Languages, organize poetry contests to familiarize students with famous literary works. Since they're competing with other children who might not be native speakers, your children will have a chance to display their language skills and feel proud to see their language valued by their community. I remember memorizing the poem "La Mort du Loup" by Alfred de Vigny for a contest in high school; although I stumbled on a line and only got second place, it broadened my horizons and marked a new way for me to learn more about French literature. In Russia, you can stop almost anyone on the street and ask them for a few lines from their beloved Alexander Pushkin; you will instantly be treated to a wonderful poetry recital. It's quite amazing.

Another idea, based on the Letters for Literature contest sponsored by the Center for the Book in the Library of Congress, is to have your child write a letter to a favorite author (who writes in his or her heritage language). You can then send the letter to the author's publishers' address. The 2008/2009 national Letters for Literature contest received more than 54,000 entries from children from grades 4 through 12, which means it's an activity that inspires children of all ages!

YOUR STATE LIBRARY

We all know libraries offer a wealth of information for the whole family. In addition to your local library, don't forget to check out your state library. You can either search its website for resources or you can contact the staff directly. Let them know what language your family speaks and how old your children are. Get ready to be amazed at how resourceful librarians can be!

The Library of Congress has developed a treasure-trove website called Global Gateway: World Cultures and Resources (http://international.loc.gov/intldl/intldlhome.html). You can search by country, and it will connect you to subjects including "Language and Literature," where you will find links to your country's national library, newspapers, magazines, dictionaries, and more.

MEET COMMUNITY LEADERS

When you meet successful bilingual citizens in your community—at a doctor's office, at city council, in a law firm, at the airport—invite them to speak at your children's school about the benefits of speaking two languages and to discuss their personal experience of growing up bilingual. It's important for children to see their languages valued and, from time to time, to hear the merits of bilingualism from someone beside their parents!

BOND WITH ELDERS

In most cultures, the generation of elders plays an important role in children's lives, passing on their wisdom and cultural knowledge to the younger generation. If you don't have older relatives living nearby, here's a "think outside the box" idea.

Contact your local retirement homes and find out if any of their residents speak your heritage language. Then ask if you can contact them directly, tell them your story, and see they are interested in meeting. You soon could be spending a great hour listening to wonderful anecdotes from someone who shares a common history.

GLOBAL YOUTH SERVICE DAY

Held every April since 2000, this event is "the largest annual celebration of young volunteers, where millions of young people in countries everywhere carry out thousands of community improvement projects." The website at www.gysd.net/involve gives you and your children ideas on how to get involved. It's a great way to engage children to take pride in their communities and feel connected to other children around the world. For children who relocate often during their child-hood, it's sometimes difficult to feel like a part of the community. This event offers them just one opportunity to engage in neighborhood projects that can empower them greatly. We all know now, with President Obama's personal story, how far community organizers can go!

WORLD LANGUAGES DAY

The Center for Language Education and Research, funded by the U.S. Department of Education, offers a free guidebook titled *Celebrating the World's Languages: A Guide to Creating a World Languages Day Event*. This publication provides a step-by-step guide to plan an exciting event for high school students to highlight the importance of cultural awareness and language skills. Teachers and community groups can download the publication at http://clear.msu.edu/clear/store/moreinfo.php?product_ID=47.

LEARN SPANISH

Worldwide, close to 350 million people speak Spanish, and it represents the primary language for over half of the population of the Western Hemisphere. If you plan on living in the U.S. permanently, there are great social and economic benefits to introducing this important language to your children. It is the second most widely spoken language in this country and it is fairly easy to learn. There are also now more and more job opportunities for people who are bilingual in Spanish and English. To make things even more appealing, research shows that it is easier for a bilingual student to pick up a third language than for a monolingual to learn a second language.

STUDY FOR A DRIVER'S LICENSE

If your child is now reading international news, there's a good chance he's also getting close to taking his driver's license exam. I hear it's a pretty stressful time in a parent's life. Through the California DMV website, you can now download and print driver's license handbooks in Armenian, Chinese, Korean, Punjabi, Russian, Spanish, Tagalog, and Vietnamese. If your child is younger, it's still fun to explore new vocabulary words as you play together with plastic cars in the living room.

THE NATIONAL MUSEUM OF LANGUAGE

The National Museum of Language opened in College Park, Maryland, in May 2008 to promote "a better understanding of language and its role in history, contemporary affairs, and the future." They offer a wealth of information and resources, from podcasts to papers to online presentations at http://languagemuseum.org. For children in particular, they offer free online activities in Gaelic, Polish, and Spanish, as well as computer games to practice German, Italian, Spanish, French, and English. Children can even sign up to join the organization Young Linguists of America, sponsored by the museum.

HELICOPTER RESCUE OPERATIONS

With prior registration, many hospitals offer free tours of their facilities to young children to acquaint them with their equipment and make them more comfortable in the hospital environment. So many languages are represented in major hospitals that, with some planning and a couple of friendly emails, you can always request a volunteer who speaks your heritage language to give you the tour. You can also sometimes get a detailed information booklet to review new vocabulary words with your children after the tour.

For example, Parker Adventist Hospital in Parker, Colorado, offers tours for children ages four to seven, with a four-foot plush Curious George leading the way! The children get to wear surgical gowns and masks and visit the emergency room, an X-ray lab, a recovery room, and sometimes even the helicopter pad.

THE NATIONAL GUARD

Contact the Public Affairs Office at your local Air National Guard to see if you can tour their facilities. There might even be an Air Refueling Wing, which offers tours of a KC-135, emergency equipment, and a fire station. Ask if they have a staff member who speaks your heritage language. If they don't, you can always serve as translator! When we did a tour of our local 157th Air Refueling Wing, I made a list of French vocabulary words that we now get to practice every time the girls take out the photo album we made of that memorable day. I picked up a few words myself, since I had never seen an *avion-ravitailleur* (tanker) up close before!

THE AQUARIUM

If you live close to a good aquarium, I recommend getting a family membership because children never get tired of such a fun visit! With prior notice, large city aquariums can help you organize a tour in your heritage language, or you can invite a local university student who wants to practice her language skills. It's easy to do a self-guided tour; just make sure you give yourself enough time to stick around for the feeding of the penguins. That alone is worth the trip! You can also inquire about a behind-the-scenes tour that will show your children how biologists take care of the animals and how the tanks are maintained.

SCIENCE CENTERS

A science center makes a great outing with children. The staff can help you find a volunteer who can give a basic tour in your heritage language, or let you take extra time after the tour to go over key words in your language. There are great opportunities to learn new vocabulary dealing with nature and the environment, technology, and space sciences, with hands-on exhibits, educational workshops, and maybe even a planetarium.

CONSTRUCTION SITES

It's true that having children makes you look at life differently. And at construction sites, too! Who knew you could spend forty-five minutes with a child at a construction site and have a great time? Bring along a drink and a snack, find a safe parking spot, and you're all set. There's so much going on I can't look up the words fast enough in my dictionary! I had never learned the word *tractopelle* (digger) or *tombereau* (dump truck) for some reason. But I've heard them enough times by now that I'll never forget them, and neither will Natasha and Sofiya!

HISTORICAL HOTELS

If you live near a historical hotel, you will surely find many languages and cultures represented in its staff. With some pre-planning, these historical hotels often offer tours to give visitors a sense of what life was like in the past when famous artists, writers, and politicians stayed as guests. You can check the Historic Hotels of America for more information. At some locations you might even get a ghost tour with stories of the hotel's haunted history.

FARMS

Regardless of which language they first speak, children seem to learn the names and sounds of animals before anything else! Most farms will accommodate small tour groups and provide a great way for you to introduce new vocabulary about a subject they already love! Many farms have small animals that children can get close to or even feed. You can also tour a dairy farm, if you live near one. You can find out about the different herds, how they're fed, and the milking systems that are used.

Think about also contacting your local SPCA (Society for the Prevention of Cruelty to Animals) for a tour to meet some local furry friends and learn about animal welfare issues. Designate a relative or a friend or find a local student who will volunteer to do the tour in your heritage language.

THE RECYCLING CENTER

See your town's recycling technology in action, up close and personal! Okay, I'll be honest: I sent my husband for that visit. But nonetheless, a great opportunity for new vocabulary words and a great lesson for the kids! They'll let you do a self-guided tour to see how cans, jars, and paper are all separated and sorted, and how they're made into something new. Perfect for inquisitive minds. You can also find educational exhibits to show your children how recycling benefits the environment.

BILINGUAL CAREERS

Whenever you meet someone new in your community who speaks two languages, find out where he or she works and if it could turn out to be an interesting place to tour with children. For example, if you meet a local dentist who speaks your heritage language, it could be a great learning opportunity to experience "a day in the life" of a dentist! The kids find out more about the profession and the dentist can tell them how his languages have helped him in his career and his day-to-day patient care. This is another opportunity where your children see their heritage language used in the world around them, and not just at home.

BILINGUAL NEWSPAPER BUREAUS

After you subscribe to a bilingual newspaper, find out if you can tour their facility. Before newspapers completely disappear! It's a great way to see the staff in action and to demonstrate how useful speaking two languages can be at work. Your children can then write a thank you note in their heritage language and send it to the editor. You can also often tour photography agencies, if you contact them ahead of time.

TELEVISION STATIONS

Contact your local television station, preferably by fax or email, to see if you can organize a tour of their facility and even watch a program being taped live! Find out if anyone on staff speaks your heritage language, who can explain to your children the benefits of being bilingual in the broadcasting industry. During your tour, you'll find out how the station runs and details about the current technology they use to make it all happen.

For example, in the San Francisco Bay area you will find the KTSF television station, which is the largest Asian-language broadcast station in the U.S. According to their website they provide news and entertainment shows to more than 2.75 million people, in 12 languages. But even if you live in a smaller town, your local television station can still offer a fascinating behind-the-scenes tour that can pique your children's curiosity!

THE COURTHOUSE

City clerks will usually have documents available in the different languages represented in the community that can make great vocabulary lists! Most city courthouses offer free tours for small groups by appointment. They will sometimes work with retired teachers or lawyers or museum guides to give the tour, so don't hesitate to inquire ahead of time about a possible foreign-language tour. You will find out the history of the building, famous cases once held, and get an overview of the judicial system. Some courthouses will let you observe a live proceeding or organize a question-and-answer session with a judge. There are also certain areas that are open to the public at any time, to explore at your own pace.

GIRL SCOUTS OF THE USA

This organization now has more than 3.7 million members in the U.S. and has groups in more than ninety countries. There are now more and more global opportunities for today's Girl Scout. The program Global Girl Scouting, for example, works "to increase girls' awareness about the world, promote cross-cultural learning opportunities, and educate girls on relevant global issues that inspire them to take action." Connected to the organization's different world centers, girls learn about different cultures and build new friendships. Each February on World Thinking Day, they work with other Girl Scouts on a global problem.

The Girl Scouts, the Boy Scouts, and similar community-based organizations promote teamwork, character-building, activities, and leadership skills and give kids a more global worldview.

KIDS TO KIDS INTERNATIONAL

This organization, which you can find at www.ktki.org/story.html, works with teachers and young children to make picture books that they send to kids around the world; the kids then send back their own drawings and pictures of themselves. The organization also sends educational supplies to schools in countries such as Afghanistan and China. Children locate these countries on a map and find out what everyday life is like for students there. They also learn which languages are spoken in each country, and they start to understand why it's useful to communicate in more than one language.

LANGUAGE LEARNER REGISTRY

The American Council on the Teaching of Foreign Languages (ACTFL) recently launched a Language Learner Registry at http://llr.actfl training.org/. All foreign language students (non-native speakers) are invited to sign up, whether you're a beginner or have achieved fluency (living in the U.S. or abroad). According to the ACTFL's website, "Registry members are paid $25 each time they are interviewed for a practice test by a Tester Trainee during a Tester Training Workshop." This registry is a fun incentive for anyone learning a foreign language, as all skill levels are needed! Participants have to be at least fifteen years old and will be contacted by email when they are needed for a practice test.

START A DUAL-LANGUAGE PROGRAM!

Megean Dawson, M.ED., the principal of West View K-8, a dual language school in Burlington, Washington, offers helpful steps to start your own dual-language program in your children's school district. Here is her advice:

1. **Examine your population**

   For starters, community members interested in advocating for a DL program need to look at the size, demographics, and statistics of their district. A large percentage of ELL (English language learners) is a good start—whether these students are Spanish-, Russian-, or Korean-experts. In the two-way immersion program (a specific DL model), at least twenty-five new kindergarteners who speak the minority language is an excellent sign of viability and sustainability.

2. **Survey the community**

   How can your community benefit from a DL program? Ask around at school board meetings, local businesses, teacher meetings, Booster Club events, and local agency front desks. How could the community grow stronger by valuing and celebrating the minority language? How could high school students, counselors, realtors, and police officers become a part of the DL team as it begins to build?

3. **Know the facts and statistics**

   Don't be alarmed when opposition and negative Letters to the Editor appear. Many people in our country are quite happy with one language and don't want to be bothered by a second. But those very people will be interested to learn that DL programs are the quickest and most affordable method of teaching English to second-language learners. And a DL program will graduate English-experts who are completely fluent in a second language! What more could you ask for? When Americans visit European families and discover that their children are working on their fourth language, they are eager to look into a DL program close to home.

4. **Research current models**

   Don't try to reinvent the wheel! Study current DL programs across the nation by visiting schools, calling principals, and emailing teachers. There are many training opportunities in regional settings for district office personnel, teachers, and parents. Ask schools about their partnerships—whether it's with a local university, business, or exchange program. DL advocates seem to come out of the woodwork!

5. **Be patient when it comes to a data return**

   Since most DL programs start in kindergarten, it will be four full years before the first cohort of DL students take state exams. And another six months before the data is sent to the principal. It seems like a long wait, but it's certainly worth the time when scores creep up (or in some cases, blast off the charts!).

The most important advice is to remain a steady supporter of multicultural, multilingual education models while researching DL. Our journey is a long, but steady, trek into a colorful, global painting for our children's future.

(Reprinted with permission from *Multilingual Living Magazine*, March/April 2008)

ENDNOTES

CHAPTER 1

1. Fred Genesee. "A Short Guide to Raising Children Bilingually." *Multilingual Living Magazine*. Retrieved on January 8, 2007 at http://www .biculturalfamily.org/backissues.html

2. Genesee

3. Ellen Bialystok. *Language Processing in Bilingual Children*. (Cambridge, UK: Cambridge University Press, 2002), p. 21.

4. Ellen Bialystok. "Effects of Bilingualism and Biliteracy on Children's Emerging Concepts of Print." *Developmental Psychology*. Vol. 33, No. 3.

5. Benedicte De Boysson-Bardies. *How Language Comes to Children: From birth to two years.* (Cambridge, MA: MIT Press, 1999), p. 178.

6. "Child Speech and Language." American Speech-Language-Hearing Association (ASLHA). Retrieved on November 3, 2008 at http://www .asha.org/public/speech/disorders/ChildSandL.htm

7. "Learning Two Languages." American Speech-Language-Hearing Association (ASLHA). Retrieved on March 10, 2009 at http://www.asha.org/ public/speech/development/BilingualChildren.htm#expectations

8. Margaret Alic. "Symptoms of Language Delay." Encyclopedia of Children's Health: Infancy through adolescence. Retrieved on November 3, 2008 at http://www.healthofchildren.com/L/Language-Delay.html

9. Laura-Ann Pettito, Ioulia Kovelman, and S.A. Baker. "Bilingual and Monolingual Brains Compared: A functional magnetic resonance imaging investigation of syntactic processing and a possible neural signature of bilingualism." *Journal of Cognitive Neuroscience*, 20 (2008): 153–169.

10. Genesee

11. Annick De Houwer. "Two or More Languages in Early Childhood: Some General Points and Practical Recommendations." Retrieved on Feb. 2, 2007 at http://www.cal.org/resources/digest/earlychild.html

12. Tracey Tokuhama-Espinosa. *Raising Multilingual Children: Foreign language acquisition and children.* (Bergin & Garvey, 2000), p. 28.

13. Colin Baker. *The Care and Education of Young Bilinguals: An introduction for professsionals.* (Clevedon, UK: Multilingual Matters, 2000), p. 2.

14. Ulrike Jessner. "Teaching Third Languages: Findings, trends, and challenges." *Language Teaching,* 41 (2008): 15.

15. Tokuhama-Espinosa, p. 28.

16. Grace M. Libardo Alvarez. "A Child's Journey to Bilingualism." *Multilingual Living Magazine.* Retrieved on January 8, 2007 at http://www.biculturalfamily.org/backissues.html

17. Theodore Andersson. "A Guide to Family Reading in Two Languages: The Preschool Years." Retrieved on January 7, 2009 at http://www.ncela.gwu.edu/pubs/classics/preschool/iv.htm

18. Tokuhama-Espinosa, p. 63.

19. "Bilingual Children More Likely To Stutter." Science Daily. Retrieved on June 27, 2008 at http://www.sciencedaily.com/releases/2008/09/080908215938.htm

20. James Au-Yeung, Peter Howell, Steve Davis, Nicole Charles, and Stevie Sackin. "UCL Survey of Bilingualism and Stuttering." (2001) Retrieved on November 15, 2008 at http://www.speech.psychol.ucl.ac.uk/Publications/PAPERS/PDF/22bilingual.pdf

21. National Stutter Association. "Notes to Listeners." Retrieved on November 12, 2008 at http://www.nsastutter.org/pdfs/newsletters/m_189.pdf

22. National Stutter Association

23. Barbara Abdelilah-Bauer. *Le Defi des Enfants Bilingues: Grandir et vivre en parlant plusieurs langues.* (Paris, France: Editions La Decouverte, 2006), p. 143.

24. Baker, p. 128.

25. Deborah Jill Chitester. "Dispelling Myths of Bilingualism." *Language Magazine,* (October 2007): 23.

26. Aurore Adamkiewicz. Yahoo Group "Multilingual Munchkins."
27. Baker, p. 137.

CHAPTER 2

1. "An Interview of Francois Grosjean on Bilingualism." Retrieved on August 2, 2007 at http://www.francoisgrosjean.ch/interview_en.html
2. U.S. Census Bureau. American FactFinder. Retrieved on February 13, 2009 at http://factfinder.census.gov/servlet/STTable?_bm=y&-geo_id=01000US&-qr_name=ACS_2007_3YR_G00_S1603&-ds_name=ACS_2007_3YR_G00_
3. Emily Alpert. "Spinning Tales in Two Languages: Questions for Irene Marquez." *Voice of San Diego.* Retrieved on September 6, 2008 at http://www.voiceofsandiego.org/articles/2008/05/10/people/982 marquez051008.txt
4. Personal correspondence
5. Fred Genesee. "A Short Guide to Raising Children Bilingually." *Multilingual Living Magazine.* Retrieved on January 8, 2007 at http://www.biculturalfamily.org/backissues.html
6. Francois Grosjean. *Life with Two Languages: An introduction to bilingualism.* (Cambridge, MA: Harvard University Press, 1982), p. 206.
7. Madalena Cruz-Ferreira. "Language Mismatches." *Multilingual Living Magazine.* Nov./Dec. 2007. Retrieved on November 14, 2008 at http://www.biculturalfamily.org/backissues.html
8. "Does Bilingualism Help Children Learn to Read?" *Early Advantage Newsletter.* Retrieved on November 11, 2008 at http://www.early-advantage.com/newsletterarchive/newsletter20071127.aspx
9. "Learning to Read." American Academy of Pediatrics. Retrieved on November 11, 2008 at http://www.aap.org/publiced/BR_Read.htm
10. John Guthrie. "Teaching for Literacy Engagement." *Journal of Literacy Research.* Retrieved on November 12, 2008 http://findarticles.com/p/articles/mi_qa3785/is_200404/ai_n9398882
11. Una Cunningham-Andersson and Staffan Andersson. *Growing Up with Two Languages: A practical guide.* (London, UK: Routledge, 2004), p. 60.

12. "Do Women Really Talk More than Men?" Physorg.com. Retrieved on November 11, 2008 at http://www.physorg.com/news102865702 .html

13. Betty Hart and Todd R. Risley. *Meaningful Differences in the Everyday Experience of Young American Children.* (Baltimore: Brookes Publishing Co., 1995).

14. Personal correspondence

15. Una Cunningham-Andersson and Staffan Andersson. *Growing Up With Two Languages: A practical guide.* (London, UK: Routledge, 2004), p. 62.

16. Personal correspondence

CHAPTER 3

1. Barbara Crossette. "U.N. Coaxes Out the Wheres and Whys of Global Immigration." *New York Times,* July 7, 2002.

2. Peter Marris. *Loss and Change.* (Garden City, NY: Anchor Press/ Doubleday, 1975), p. 19.

3. Jim Cummins. *Language, Power, and Pedagogy: Bilingual children in the crossfire.* (Clevedon, UK: Multilingual Matters, 2003), p. 38.

4. Pauline Gibbons. *Learning to Learn in a Second Language.* (Newtown, Australia: Primary English Teaching Association, 1991), p. 3.

5. Cummins, p. 34.

6. Donaldo Macedo. *Literacies of Power: What Americans are not allowed to know.* (Boulder, CO: Westview Press, 1994), p. 1.

7. Otto Santa-Ana. (Ed.). *Tongue-Tied: The lives of multilingual children in public education.* (Lanham, MD: Rowman and Littlefield Publishers, Inc., 2004), p. 6.

8. Mariana Souto-Manning. "A Critical Look at Bilingualism Discourse in Public Schools: Autoethnographic Reflections of a Vulnerable Observer," *Bilingual Research Journal,* (Summer 2006): 573.

9. Jim Cummins. "Teaching Language for Learning." *Language Magazine,* (August 2008), p. 25.

10. Francois Grosjean. *Life with Two Languages: An introduction to bilingualism.* (Cambridge, MA: Harvard University Press, 1932), p. 67.

11. Dugan Romano. *Intercultural Marriage: Promises and pitfalls.* 2d ed. (Yarmouth, ME: Intercultural Press, 2001), p. 128.

12. Hisham Motkal Abu-Rayya. "Ethnic Self-Identification and Psychological Well-Being among Adolescents with European Mothers and Arab Fathers in Israel." *International Journal of Intercultural Relations,* 30 (2006): 545–556.

13. Personal correspondence

14. Harriet Cannon, "Your Cultural Identity Changes As Your Child Grows." *Multilingual Living Magazine.* Retrieved on March 1, 2008 at http://www.biculturalfamily.org/backissues.html

15. "A New Language Barrier: Why learning a new language may make you forget your old one." Science Daily. Retrieved on August 20, 2008 at http://www.sciencedaily.com/releases/2007/01/070118094015.htm

16. Stephen D. Krashen. *Condemned Without a Trial: Bogus arguments against bilingual education.* (Portsmouth, NH: Heinemann, 1999), p. ix.

17. Colin Baker. Waltham Forest Bilingual Group. Retrieved on February 14, 2007 at http://www.wfbilingual.org.uk/pages/speakers/colin/colin baker.html

CHAPTER 4

1. Geert Hoefstede. *Culture's Consequences: International differences in work-related issues.* (Beverly Hills, CA: Sage, 1980)

2. Alberto E. Fantini. *Language Acquisition of a Bilingual Child.* (Brattleboro, VT: The Experiment Press, 1974), p. 46.

3. Sandra Whitehead. "Bicultural Families: Meeting the Challenges of Raising Children with Two Cultures." Parenthood.com. Retrieved on Feb. 5, 2007 at http://www.parenthood.com/article-topics/bicultural_families_ meeting_the_challenges_of_raising_children_with_two_cultures.html

4. Personal correspondence

5. Personal correspondence

6. J. Steven Reznick. "Intelligence, Language, Nature, and Nurture in Young Twins." *Intelligence, Heredity, and Environment,* edited by Robert J. Sternberg and Elena Grigorenko. (Cambridge, UK: Cambridge University Press, 1997)

7. "Preparing for Multiples." National Organization of Mothers of Twins Clubs. Retrieved on Feb. 11, 2008 at http://www.nomotc.org/index.php?option=com_content&task=view&id=52&Itemid=51

8. Svenka Savic. *How Twins Learn to Talk.* (London, UK: Academic Press, 1980)

9. Modern Language Association. Language Map. Retrieved on Feb. 5, 2007 at http://www.mla.org/map_main

10. "Fact Sheet on the Foreign Born." Migration Policy Institute. Retrieved on February 13, 2009 at http://www.migrationinformation.org/datahub/acscensus.cfm#

11. Annick De Houwer. "Two or More Languages in Early Childhood: Some General Points and Practical Recommendations." Center for Applied Linguistics. Retrieved on Feb. 2, 2007 at http://www.cal.org/resources/digest/earlychild.html

12. Fred Genesee. "A Short Guide to Raising Kids Bilingually." *Multilingual Living Magazine.* Retrieved on January 8, 2007 at http://www.biculturalfamily.org/backissues.html

13. Traute Taeschner. *The Sun is Feminine: A study on language acquisition in bilingual children.* (Berlin, Germany: Springer-Verlag, 1983), p. 192.

14. Personal correspondence

15. Taeschner, p. 205.

16. Taeschner, p. 209.

CHAPTER 5

1. U.S. Department of Education, National Center for Education Statistics. "1.5 Million Homeschooled Students in the United States in 2007." Retrieved on January 28, 2009 at http://nces.ed.gov/pubs2009/2009030.pdf

2. Lindsey M. Burke. "Homeschooling Sees Dramatic Rise in Popularity." Heritage Foundation. Retrieved on January 28, 2009 at http://www.heritage.org/Research/Education/wm2254.cfm

3. "Questions to a Homeschooler: An Interview with Corey Heller." *Multilingual Living Magazine.* Nov./Dec. 2007. Retrieved on at http://www.biculturalfamily.org/backissues.html

4. Personal correspondence
5. "Two Way Immersion." Center for Applied Linguistics. Retrieved on January 28, 2009 at http://www.cal.org/twi/
6. Center for Applied Linguistics
7. Stephen Krashen. English First. "Bilingual Education: Ninety questions, ninety answers." Retrieved on January 25, 2009 at http://www.english-first.org/be/be90krashen.htm.
8. Wayne E.Wright. "Heritage Language Programs in the Era of English-Only and No Child Left Behind." *Heritage Language Journal.* Retrieved on January 10, 2009 at http://www.international.ucla.edu/languages/heritagelanguages/journal/print.asp?parentid=56454
9. Shuhan C. Wang and Nancy Green. "Heritage Language Students in the K–12 Education System" in *Heritage Languages in America: Preserving a national resource*, edited by J.K. Peyton, Donald A. Ranard, and Scott McGinnis (Washington, D.C.: Center for Applied Linguistics, 2001), pp. 177–178.
10. Alliance for the Advancement of Heritage Languages. "Core Principles of the Alliance." Retrieved on January 28, 2009 at http://www.cal.org/heritage/about/principles.html
11. Sara Rimer. "Immigrants in Charter Schools Are Seeking the Best of Both Worlds." *New York Times*, January 9, 2009.
12. U.S Charter Schools. "Overview." Retrieved on January 29, 2009 at http://www.uscharterschools.org/pub/uscs_docs/o/index.htm
13. Marjukka Grover. *Bilingual Family Newsletter.* 2005, Vol. 22, No. 4.

CHAPTER 6

1. Charles Taylor. *Multiculturalism: Examining the politics of recognition.* (Princeton, NJ: Princeton University Press, 1994), p. 26.
2. Judith M. Blohm and Terri Lapinsky. *Kids Like Me: Voices of the immigrant experience.* (Yarmouth, ME: Intercultural Press, 2006), p. 99.
3. Stephen Krashen. "Bilingual Education: Ninety questions, ninety answers." Retrieved on January 7, 2008 at http://www.englishfirst.org/be/be90krashen.htm

4. Krashen

5. Francesco Cavallaro. "Language Maintenance Revisited: An Australian perspective." *Bilingual Research Journal*. Retrieved on September 15, 2008 at http://www3.ntu.edu.sg/home/CFCavallaro/Research.htm

6. Presidential Campaign. Town Hall Meeting, Powder Springs, GA. July 8, 2008.

7. U.S. Census Bureau. American FactFinder. Retrieved on February 13, 2009 at http://factfinder.census.gov/servlet/STTable?_bm=y&-geo_id= 01000US&-qr_name=ACS_2007_3YR_G00_S1603&-ds_name=ACS_ 2007_3YR_G00_

8. Pico Pyer. "My Chance Encounter with Obama in Hawaii." Retrieved on November 25, 2008 at http://news.yahoo.com/s/time/20081108/us_ time/mychanceencounterwithobamainhawaii

9. Frank McCourt. *Angela's Ashes*. (New York, NY: Scribner, 1999)

10. Colin Baker. *The Care and Education of Young Bilinguals: An introduction for professionals*. (Clevedon, UK: Multilingual Matters, 2000), p. 127.

11. Ruben G. Rumbaut. U.S. Judiciary Committee. Retrieved on August 14, 2007 at http://www.boston.com/news/local/articles/2007/07/22/ immigrant_parents_struggle_to_keep_their_children_bilingual/

12. Nataly Kelly. "Caught In The Grips of Linguistic Paranoia." *International Herald Tribune*, August 11, 2008.

13. Jodi Kantor. "Nation's Many Faces in Extended First Family." *New York Times*, January 21, 2009.

14. Rey M. Rodriguez. "Is Your Spanish Hurting Their English?" *LA Language World*. Retrieved on September 8, 2008 at http://www.lalamag .ucla.edu/features/article.asp?parentid=74511

15. J. Michael Adams and Angelo Carfagna. *Coming of Age in a Globalized World*. (Bloomfield, CT: Kumarian Press, 2006), p. 5.

16. Rick Fry and Felisa Gonzales. "One-in-Five and Growing Fast: A profile of Hispanic public school students." Pew Hispanic Center. Retrieved on November 21, 2008 at http://www.pewhispanic.org

17. Jim Cummins. *Negotiating Identities: Education for Empowerment in a Diverse Society*. (California Association for Bilingual Education, 2001), p. 225.

18. "A Call to Action for National Foreign Language Capabilities." National Language Conference. Retrieved on April 2, 2008 at http://www.nl conference.org/docs/White_Paper.pdf

19. J. K. Peyton, Donald A. Ranard, & Scott McGinnis. (Eds.). *Heritage Languages in America: Preserving a national resource.* (Washington, D.C.: Center for Applied Linguistics, 2001), back cover.

20. "Maryland Takes National Lead to Preserve Foreign Language Assets." Maryland State Department of Education. Retrieved on June 23, 2009 at http://www.marylandpublicschools.org/NR/exeres/6412C80C-B1DF-4D8E-92AC-7D9C59AB09B4,frameless.htm?Year=2009&Month=2%%3E

21. Victor C. Johnson and Janice Mulholland. "Open Doors, Secure Borders: Advantages of Education Abroad for Public Policy." International Educator. May/June 2006. Retrieved on November 12, 2008 at http://www.nafsa.org/_/File/_/mayjun.pdf

22. "New MLA Survey Shows Significant Increases in Foreign Language Study at U.S. Colleges and Universities." Modern Language Association. Retrieved on January 12, 2008 at http://www.mla.org/pdf/release11207_ma_feb_update.pdf

23. "Legislative Highlights." Joint National Committee for Languages and the National Council for Languages and International Studies. Retrieved on June 23, 2009 at http://www.languagepolicy.org/legislation/index.html

24. "National Language Service Corps Hosts Meeting of Charter Members." National Language Service Corps. Retrieved on June 23, 2009 at http://www.nationallanguageservicecorps.org

CHAPTER 7

1. Ellen Bialystok. *Bilingualism in Development: Language, literacy, and cognition.* (Cambridge, UK: Cambridge University Press, 2001).

2. "The Bilingual Brain." Brain Briefings. Society for Neuroscience. September 2008. Retrieved on January 9, 2009 at http://www.sfn.org/index.cfm?pagename=brainbriefings_thebilingualbrain

3. Suzanne Flynn. "The Benefits of Bilingualism." Lecture presented on May 4, 2006 at the German International School in Boston, MA. Retrieved at http://www.makingmusik.com/servlet/KM_Display Page?p=bilingualism&s=3162

4. Carolyn Kessler and Mary Ellen Quinn. "Positive Effects of Bilingualism on Science Problem-Solving Abilities," in *Georgetown University Round Table on Languages and Linguistics,* edited by James E. Alatis, (Washington, DC: Georgetown University Press, 1980): 295–308.

5. College Board. 2007 College-Bound Seniors: Total Group Profile Report. Retrieved on February 28, 2009 at http://www.collegeboard.com/ prod_downloads/about/news_info/cbsenior/yr2007/national-report.pdf

6. J. Michael Adams and Angelo Carfagna. *Coming of Age in a Globalized World.* (Bloomfield, CT: Kumarian Press, 2006), p. xii.

7. Maria Pilar Sagasta Errasti. "Acquiring Writing Skills in a Third Language: The positive effects of bilingualism." *International Journal of Bilingualism.* Retrieved on February 13, 2009 at http://ijb.sagepub.com/cgi/ content/abstract/7/1/27

8. "Education for Global Leadership: The importance of international studies and foreign language education for U.S. Economic and National Security." Committee for Economic Development. Retrieved on April 12, 2008 at http://www.ced.org/images/library/reports/education/report_ foreignlanguages.pdf

9. U.S. Census Bureau. American FactFinder. Retrieved on February 13, 2009 at http://factfinder.census.gov/servlet/STTable?_bm=y&-geo_id= 01000US&-qr_name=ACS_2007_3YR_G00_S1603&-ds_name=ACS_ 2007_3YR_G00_

10. "A Call to Action for National Foreign Language Capabilities." National Language Conference. Retrieved on April 2, 2008 at http://www.nl conference.org/docs/White_Paper.pdf

11. "Languages of USA." Ethnologue: Languages of the world. Retrieved on February 13, 2009 at http://www.ethnologue.org/show_country.asp? name=US

12. "Languages and Cultures." William Paterson University. Retrieved on April 15, 2008 at http://www.wpunj.edu/career/careersin_languages.htm

13. Stella Ting-Toomey. *Communicating Across Cultures*. (New York, NY: The Guilford Press, 1999), p. 16.

CHAPTER 8

Joshua A. Fishman. "What Do You Lose When You Lose Your Language?" in G. Cantoni (Ed.) *Stabilizing Indigenous Languages*. (Flagstaff, AZ: Center for Excellence in Education, Northern Arizona University, 1996)

Catherine Snow and Charles A. Ferguson. *Talking to Children: Language Input and Acquisition.* (New York, NY: Cambridge University Press, 1979).

Xiaoxia Li. "How Can Language Minority Parents Help Their Children Become Bilingual In Familial Context? A Case Study of a Language Minority Mother and her Daughter." *Bilingual Research Journal.*

Gordon J. Douglas. "Hablemos Espanol en Casa," The New Mexico Association for Bilingual Education website. http://www.nmabe.net/nmabe_publications/we_speak_spanish.html

Stephen Krashen. "Ending All Literacy Crises," *Language Magazine*, May 2008.

Theodore Andersson. *A Guide to Family Reading in Two Languages: The Preschool Years.* (Austin, TX: University of Texas Press, 1981)

Rey M. Rodriguez. "Won't Your Spanish Hurt Their English?" *LA Language World.* July 2007.

Julia Alvarez. "Writers on America." U.S. Department of State. International Information Programs. http://usa.usembassy.de/etexts/writers/alvarez.htm

Craig Storti. *The Art of Crossing Cultures*. (Boston, MA: Intercultural Press, 2007)

Robin Pascoe. *Raising Global Nomads: Parenting Abroad in an On-Demand World.* (Expatriate Press Limited, 2006)

Harriet Cannon. "Your Cultural Identity Changes As Your Child Grows." *Multilingual Living magazine.* March/April 2007

Judith Ortiz Cofer. Answers.com website

H. Ned Seelye and Jacqueline Howell Wasilewski. *Between Cultures: Developing Self-Identity in a World of Diversity.* (Lincolnwood, IL: NTC Publishing Group, 1996)

Colin Baker. *The Care and Education of Young Bilinguals: An introduction to professionals.* (Clevedon, UK: Multilingual Matters, 2005)

Elizabeth Pathy Salett, Diane R. Koslow, and Elsie Achugbue. (2003). *Race, Ethnicity and Self: Identity in Multicultural Perspective.* National Multicultural Institute.

Katy Abel. "Inventing Identities: Raising Multicultural Kids." *Family Education.* http://life.familyeducation.com/multiculturalism/parenting/36268.html

Barbara F. Schaetti and Sheila J. Ramsey. "The Global Nomad Experience: Living in Liminality." Transition Dynamics website.

Teresa Bevin. "Bilingual Writer and Educator. Escritora y Educadora Bilingue." Teresa Bevin website.

Dugan Romano. *Intercultural Marriage: Promises and Pitfalls.* (Boston, MA: Intercultural Press, 1997)

Vivien Stewart. "Becoming Citizens of the World." *Educational Leadership.* April 2007

Andreas Schleicher. "The Economics of Knowledge: Why Education is Key for Europe's Success, *Lisbon Council Policy Brief*, 2006.

Daniel Meiland. "In Search of Global Leaders." *Harvard Business Review.* August 1, 2003.

Wayne P. Thomas and Virginia P. Collier. (2001). *School Effectiveness for Language Minority Students.* Berkeley, CA: Center for Research on Education, Diversity & Excellence. U.S. Department of Education.

Jim Cummins. *Negotiating Identities: Education for Empowerment in a Diverse Society.* Covina, (CA: California Association for Bilingual Education, 2001)

García, Ofelia. *Bilingual Education in the 21st Century: A global perspective.* (West Sussex: UK: Wiley-Blackwell, 2009)

Stephen May. (2008). *Language and Minority Rights: Ethnicity, nationalism and the politics of language.* New York, NY: Routledge.

Daniel Ward. Editorial. *Language magazine.* October 2008.

J.A. Fishman. "300-Plus Years of Heritage Language Education in the United States," in Joy Kreeft Peyton, Donald A. Ranard, & Scott McGinnis. (Eds.). *Heritage Languages in America: Preserving a national resource.* (Washington, D.C.: Center for Applied Linguistics, 2001)

INDEX